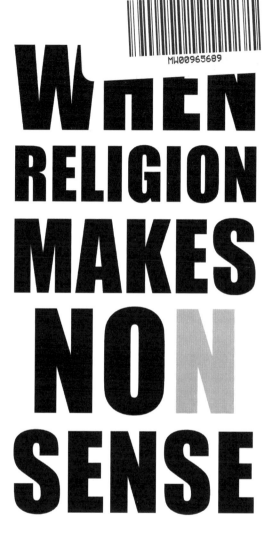

WHEN RELIGION MAKES NONSENSE

Biblical Answers for
Tough Universal Questions

Martha M. Wiebe

WHEN RELIGION MAKES NO(N) SENSE
Biblical Answers for Tough Universal Questions

Printed in Canada
ISBN: 978-1-77069-272-5

Word Alive Press
131 Cordite Road, Winnipeg, MB R3W 1S1
www.wordalivepress.ca

MIX
Paper from
responsible sources
FSC
www.fsc.org
FSC® C016245

Library and Archives Canada Cataloguing in Publication

Wiebe, Martha M. (Martha Marie), 1967-
    When religion makes no(n) sense / Martha M. Wiebe.
ISBN 978-1-77069-272-5

    1. Christianity. 2. Bible--Theology. I. Title.
    II. Title: When religion makes no sense.
    III. Title: When religion makes nonsense.

BR121.3.W54 2011   230   C2011-902217-6

DEDICATION

THIS BOOK IS DEDICATED, FIRST OF ALL, TO MY LORD and Saviour Jesus Christ, who has inspired me and guided me, by means of the Holy Spirit, to share with others what He has so graciously shared with me.

This book is also dedicated to my husband, Abe, and our four wonderful children and their spouses—Jeremy and Tabitha, Kevin and Emily, Lawrence and Angie, and Marcella. They have been a great encouragement and support to me.

I also want to dedicate this work to the many people who have inspired me by asking challenging questions and making statements which prompted me to research various subjects for the book.

Thanks to my mom, whose faith in Jesus has been a positive example in my life. She also encouraged me to think for myself, and promoted education in our family. Thanks also to Dad, who loved the Lord dearly, showed God's love to others, and whose last words to me were, "Hold onto Jesus."

Special thanks to everyone who encouraged me to write, and asked about the work-in-progress along the way. I think especially of Judy Clarke, Joy Hewitt-Smith, Roy Beniston, Sarah

Krahn, Lynda Washkevich, Eva Wiebe, Tina Neudorf, and Lisa Douglas. Special thanks also to Leigh Shaheen, my writing instructor (and encourager) from Long Ridge Writer's Group, and to John Kostelyk, who first planted the thought of writing in my head. I once shared something at church that I wrote, and during coffee after the service John asked me, "When will you start writing?" Thanks also to our current church family, Faith Gospel Fellowship, for being a continuous source of blessing and encouragement week after week. Thanks to Ken and Sandra, for being the first to proofread the finished product. Thanks for all your prayers and encouragement, dear family in Christ! God Bless you all!

CONTENTS

FOREWORD

THE CHAPTERS IN THIS BOOK DISCUSS SOME OF THE questions raised through the following fictional story, which portrays many of the real-life issues that people struggle with everyday. Does staying true to your faith mean that you have to stay part of the same congregation all your life? How can a searching unbeliever know which church to go to, or which Bible to buy? Where can we find answers when we're confused about what we've learned?

I don't have all the answers, but through searching the Scriptures, and through revelations given me by the Holy Spirit, I have found comfort and gained insight from God's Word in many of these areas. However, I also challenge you not to take my word for it. Rather, look up each reference for yourself, and use a concordance to research additional scripture passages on each subject. My concordance has been an indispensable tool in my research and Bible study; it helps me find the verses I only vaguely remember. I want to share some of my findings with you in the hopes that you will experience God's love and grow a strong desire to know Him better through His Word as you find yourself falling in love with Jesus Christ. God Bless!

INTRODUCTION

FAITHFUL AND TRUE

DAVEHADNEVERBEENTOCHURCH.HISPARENTSHAD never taken him, even though they were members at his grandparents' church, about two hundred kilometers away. When he was younger, Dave's friends had sometimes invited him to visit their churches, but Dave had never been allowed to go. Mom and Dad had said that Grandma and Grandpa would not be pleased if they found out they were allowing their son to forsake his own faith. Dave's parents only went to church when they went to visit Grandma and Grandpa at Christmas and Easter, and for the occasional wedding or funeral. On these occasions, an older cousin often volunteered to babysit, as the church service was long and not really meant for children. When Dave got older, his parents quit going altogether and he would overhear them talking about the hypocrisy within the church and how they wanted no part of it.

When Dave was sixteen, he started socializing with the drinking crowd. They often had parties at each other's homes and experimented with drugs and alcohol when their parents were out of town. This lifestyle seemed to be normal for teenagers, almost like this was what the community expected of them. Many believed that young people needed to have a wild, rebellious life before they could be capable of settling down to become responsible adults.

This same lifestyle continued as Dave grew up, got a job, and left home. He roomed together with his girlfriend Becky so that they could share expenses. It was only after Becky got pregnant that Dave started thinking about taking life seriously. What were they going to teach their baby when it arrived? It looked like a huge responsibility. Dave and Becky talked about it and decided to get married. After all, they loved each other and their baby would need good role models and a stable home environment. They decided to visit Dave's parents and tell them the good news.

"So when and where is this exciting event taking place?" asked Dave's dad, who seemed more thrilled about the news than his mom.

"We arranged a date with the judge at the courthouse for June 15," said Becky. "We're having a small reception at my parents' place for family and close friends. It will be a barbecue, and we can use the garage if it rains."

"But what about getting baptized, joining a church, and getting married there?" protested Dave's mom, who hadn't said a word until now. "What I mean is, a courthouse is no place for a wedding! People will think we didn't teach you anything!"

"Now, now, dear," cautioned Dave's dad. "You know as well as I do that the only reason you and I joined the church was because it was the only way we could get married with your parents' approval. Remember, we always said we would never force rules on our children that we couldn't understand ourselves."

"I remember," relented Mom. "However, you also know that my parents won't come to the wedding unless it's at their church. You know how set in their ways they are."

"I know," said Dad. "But I really don't care anymore. We can't let their opinions hurt our children as they have hurt us. Personally, I'm very proud of Dave and Becky for choosing to be responsible adults and parents. The way our government is set up, they could live common-law forever and have the same benefits married couples do. They could also abort all our grandchildren, compliments of Alberta Health Care, and nobody would ever know the difference."

"I'm proud of you, too," whispered Mom, with tears in her voice, "and I'm sorry for my attitude. I have just never understood why these things are so complicated. Let us know what we can do to help with the wedding."

Although wedding plans were proceeding and everything was going as planned, Dave was troubled. Why had Mom said those things about church? What was baptism? Why had his parents quit attending church, and why hadn't they taught him about it, if it was important? He suddenly remembered how frustrated his dad had been a few years ago when he and Mom had quit attending the occasional church service. Dad had been into reading his Bible in those days, and had been very confused by the differences between what God's Word said and what the church taught.

He remembered a specific occasion when Dad had come home from a meeting with a pastor and called it quits. He could still hear Dad's words: "I can't believe it! I showed the pastor scripture from the Bible that we as a church should use to deal with situations such as the Jones one, but he just kept on saying that the church has always done things this way, and they weren't about to change. It seems like church is just a club for the perfect, and if they treat people like they treated the Jones family, I want no part of it!"

As Dave pondered these thoughts, he decided that he really should invest in a Bible. He knew that with the wedding and baby coming up, he really didn't have extra money to spend. However, he decided to check out the bookstore, and was delighted when he found a Bible on their discount table for less than half the regular price.

Over the next few weeks, Dave started reading his Bible more and more. He started in the New Testament and was quite impressed with its main character—Jesus. Was it really possible for someone to love as much as Jesus had? Was it really true that God cared about and knew how many hairs he had on his head? If this was true, then God cared much more about Dave than Dave cared about himself.

The story about the prodigal son in Luke 15 really touched his heart. Jesus used this story as an example to explain how much God loves repentant sinners and welcomes them into His family with open arms. Was it possible that Jesus loved him? It was overwhelming and he decided to make the two-hour trip to his grandparents' church the following Sunday. Just maybe someone there would be able to explain things to him.

Dave was a few minutes late for the church service, and the congregation was already singing as he walked in. As he looked for a seat, he could feel the people just looking at him. He suddenly felt very self-conscious. His jeans and t-shirt felt like rags as he noticed how all the other men were dressed in their Sunday suits. The singing was comforting, though, reminding him of the songs Mom had sung when he was little. The sermon that followed was about Jesus' love for all mankind, and Dave felt sure that someone would be able to answer his questions.

After the service was over, Dave made his way across the foyer to speak to the pastor who had delivered the morning message. He was a bit nervous as he approached him, but started talking about his interest in Jesus and asked the pastor if it was true that God loves, forgives, and accepts repentant sinners into His family. "If this is true," Dave said nervously, "then my girlfriend and I would like to live for Him, become part of your church, and get married here. I know it would mean a lot to my mom if we belonged to the same church that her and Dad do."

"Well," said the pastor, "while it's true that God accepts repentant sinners the way they are when they come to Him, we still have to please people. The leadership in this church has put rules in place to ensure that all members live up to certain standards. In order for you to become a part of our church, you first have to prove that you truly are a changed person. We have a membership class, which will prepare you to be a member here. We expect you to abstain from everything sinful, and we have a dress code. After you have completed the membership class, and the congregation has gotten to know you, we have a membership meeting and vote to see if we all agree to accept you as a member."

"I'll think about it," said Dave, crestfallen. He suddenly had a lot of respect for his parents, and felt a surge of compassion for his dad. He now knew why they had quit church. The sad thing was that they had also given up on the Bible.

Later that week, Becky's Uncle Joe came over for coffee. The conversation turned to the subject of church, and Dave shared his recent excitement about God's love for sinners from Luke 15. Uncle Joe glanced over Dave's shoulder and interrupted Dave's reading.

"Which Bible are you reading from, Dave?" he asked.

Dave handed the Bible to him. "Just a regular Holy Bible I guess. The bookstore had them for a very good price."

"This is the wrong Bible, Dave," said Uncle Joe as he looked at the cover. "Has nobody ever told you which Bible is the right one?"

Dave was quite depressed after Uncle Joe left. If his Bible wasn't true, then the stories about Jesus must also be a lie. If the Bible couldn't be trusted, then what could he trust? After all, Uncle Joe had been a baptized church member for many years who faithfully attended Bible study every Wednesday. Surely he knew what he was talking about. He might as well give up on this whole idea. His parents were right; the church and everything associated with it was very confusing and hypocritical.

It was fifteen years later before Dave picked up his Bible again, when their oldest daughter started asking questions. It was then that they decided to try a few different churches, finding one that practiced the love that Dave had read about in the Gospel so many years before. Dave and Becky and their children eventually all accepted the free gift of salvation through the grace of God, which Jesus died for on the cross of Calvary and offers to everyone.

Dave's parents were happy for them, and his dad started reading the Bible again. His mom went back to attending her parent's church occasionally, although Dad wouldn't go with her. Dave and Becky found scripture references stating the fact that all believers of Jesus Christ are one family, no matter their nationality or culture. This family includes any denomination that proclaims Jesus as Lord.

Dave's dad wanted to try other congregations, but then Mom wouldn't come, and he didn't want to go without her. Mom said she wanted to stay true to the faith her parents had taught her, which meant she could never visit other congregations. She knew what they said about people who did that; she had heard enough gossip about church-hoppers when she was a child, and her heart had always hurt for the people being talked about. Besides, keeping her membership where it was gave her a sense of security, knowing that her funeral would be looked after someday. The pastor always complimented the deceased when they had stayed true to their church, even if that person had hardly ever come. Since Dave's mom had minimal education, she couldn't understand when her husband, children, and grandchildren tried to share Bible truths with her.

Today, Dave and Becky and their family are still excited about Jesus, and are busy loving their neighbours as themselves, including unbelieving family members. They know that just preaching isn't enough to draw them to Jesus Christ. Only God can draw them through the Holy Spirit, and the love of Christians helps the process. They know that the actions of Christians are often the only Bible that unbelievers read. They try hard to live upright moral lives of integrity so that they aren't a stumbling block to others coming to the saving grace of Jesus Christ. They have faith that, in God's time, their loved ones will all know Christ. All they can do is pray and follow Jesus' example of loving others and continue sharing God's Word as the Lord leads and inspires them.

HOMEWORK

The characters in this story unfortunately did not know their Bibles very well. Read the following Scripture passages and find out how following the Bible's teaching would have saved all of them from much heartache. What happens when people are turned away from Jesus and don't have another opportunity to find out that He does, in fact, love them? Whose responsibility is it, according to Scripture?

- Scriptures about the family of God (being one in Christ with all other believers): *Matthew 12:46–50; Mark 9:38–41; 1 Corinthians 3:1–11; 1 Corinthians 12:3,12–31; Galatians 3:26–29; and Colossians 3:11.*

- Scriptures about how to treat children (possibly also young believers or searching unbelievers): *Matthew 18:1–6; Mark 9:33–37; Mark 10:13–16; Luke 10:21; and Luke 18:15–17.*

- What is our responsibility as believers, disciples, teachers, shepherds, and pastors? *Ezekiel 34; Isaiah 58; Matthew 7:12; Matthew 23; Matthew 25:31–46; Matthew 28:19–20; Mark 16:15–20; John 13:34–35; 1 Peter 5:1–4; and Hebrews 13:1–17.*

- Who did Jesus come for? *Matthew 9:9–13; Matthew 11:18–19; Matthew 18:10–14; Matthew 21:14–16; Luke 15; Luke 18:9–14; Luke 19:1–10; and Acts 2:38–40.*

CHAPTER ONE

YOU ARE CHOSEN

I LAY TOSSING AND TURNING IN MY BED. I DARED not go to sleep. What if I should die during the night? What if I wake up in hell? How could a person possibly be good enough to go to heaven? How bad did someone have to be to inherit hell?

Have you ever wondered about heaven and hell, and had restless nights like I did? Have you ever picked up a Bible and read some of it to see what it's about? Have you wondered if there really is a God and how it might possibly affect you? If you have ever thought about these things, and have an unfulfilled void inside you, then you are chosen by God.

The questions and thoughts we have which wonder about God are inspired by the Holy Spirit, prompting us to call out to Him. Jesus said, *"No one can come to me unless the Father who sent me draws him… and [enables] him"* (John 6:44,65). Sooner or later, He draws everyone, because He is not willing that anyone should perish, but wants everyone to come to repentance (2 Peter 3:9). When the Holy Spirit is sent by the Father to draw someone to Himself, He causes the soul of the individual to search in a restless way for true meaning in life. At this time, people often become believers as they repent from their sins and receive Jesus Christ as Saviour and Lord (John 1:12). They ask and receive, seek and find, and when they knock the door is opened to them (Matthew 7:7–8).

My son Kevin was quite troubled when the Lord drew him to Himself when he was about ten years old. He had invited Jesus to come live in his heart as a young child, had always come to church with us, and believed what we taught him. Kevin came to me one day and said, "Mom, I know I shouldn't say this, but I sometimes wonder if God is real. How is it possible that He always existed, and… where did He come from?"

Kevin was feeling guilty for doubting what he had been taught. I reassured him that God wasn't mad at him, and that God loved him. I was able to explain how God was drawing him to Himself, and how he was chosen by God.

God did not make cookie-cutter people who would automatically love Him, believe in Him, worship Him, and glorify Him. He did not make robots to mechanically do His will and obediently follow His leading and guidance. He gave us the freedom to choose Him or reject Him. When we start wondering if God is real, He is calling us personally to come and find out. He's drawing us to Himself in order to have a Father-child relationship with us, because He wants to be real and personal to every individual. God doesn't have grandchildren—only sons and daughters. We have to accept His free gift of salvation for ourselves. We can't tag along on our parents' apron strings of faith and be saved.

A former pastor of ours used to welcome people to church on Sunday morning by saying, "Welcome to the house of the

Lord! You are not here today because you felt like crawling out of bed and being somewhere this morning. You are not here by accident. You are here today because God loves you and has chosen you to follow Him, and is drawing you closer to Himself!"

How awesome and true this is! The Bible tells us that God chose us in Him before the creation of the world! He predestined us to be adopted as His sons through Jesus Christ, who died for our sins. Because of His shed blood, we have been forgiven! (Ephesians 1:4–14 and 1 Peter 1:1–2)

So how do we become God's children? How do we get from wondering who He is, if He really exists, and why He might possibly care about us to being confident believers, secure in knowing that our Father loves us? What does it mean to repent and receive forgiveness? How can we stop fearing death and hell and look forward to eternal life in our future home in heaven?

The fact is, we have all been born into sin. Since Adam and Eve committed the first sin, we have all inherited a sinful nature. Both Jews and Gentiles alike are under sin. No one is righteous and does good, because all have sinned and have fallen short of the glory of God (Romans 3:9–23 and 5:12–19) There is nothing we can do to change this fact. Our sinful nature is genetically inherited. We are born sinners.

The good news is that God provided a remedy. The Bible tells us, *"For God so loved the world [us] that he gave his one and only Son [Jesus], that whoever believes in him shall not perish [shall not go to hell] but have eternal life"* (John 3:16). This is a promise of heaven to come. *"For God did not send his Son into the world to condemn the world, but to save the world through him. Whoever believes in him is not condemned, but whoever does not believe stands condemned already because he has not believed in the name of God's one and only Son"* (John 3:17–18).

Belief in Jesus and His finished work on the cross is the only way to heaven! It doesn't matter how good we've been, or how many bad things we've done. Jesus died for our sins, and His atoning blood is the only sacrifice that makes us righteous enough for heaven. *"For it is by grace you have been saved, through faith—and this not from yourselves, it is the gift of God—not by works, so that no one can boast"* (Ephesians 2:8–9). Jesus came for sinners (Matthew 9:10–13), and there is great rejoicing in heaven and among the angels of God whenever a sinner repents (Luke 15:7–10). This is the good news of the Gospel! Jesus died and rose again to save us from sin, so we can look forward to heaven!

There is a major difference between religion and Christianity. Religion involves men trying to somehow be good enough to go to heaven someday, making all kinds of efforts to do good deeds and make right choices, but still never knowing for sure where they stand with God. One example of this type of religion is the message that says, "Get ready to meet your God—but you can never know for sure if you have done this or not." In Christianity, we realize how sinful we really are, and how we will never be good enough ourselves. We therefore believe the good news of the Bible, which tells us that Jesus paid it all and we are forgiven by His shed blood, if we only ask for and accept His free gift of salvation. *"Yet to all who received him, to those who believed in his name, he gave the right to become children of God"* (John 1:12).

The Bible puts it quite plainly. John wrote, *"And this is the testimony: God has given us eternal life, and this life is in his Son. He who has the Son has life; he who does not have the Son of God does not have life. I write these things to you who believe in the name of the Son of God so that you may know that you have eternal life"* (1 John 5:11–13). Notice the past and present tense in this passage. It's not a future promise of someday, or maybe—if you're good enough. God has given us eternal life. We already have it, but only those who believe in Jesus Christ. Those who have Christ have eternal life. There is no doubt.

What does it mean to repent? Repentance means feeling deep regret or sorrow for one's sins and reforming one's life. It means saying sorry for what we've done wrong and resolving in our hearts to desire better next time. God knows the moment this happens, as it is a decision that takes place deep within our hearts. He is the One who searches our hearts and knows all things (Romans 8:27 and Hebrews 4:12–13).

I love the account of the thief on the cross beside Jesus:

> One of the criminals who hung there hurled insults at him: "Aren't you the Christ? Save yourself and us!"
>
> But the other criminal rebuked him. "Don't you fear God," he said, "since you are under the same sentence? We are punished justly, for we are getting what our deeds deserve. But this man has done nothing wrong." Then he said, "Jesus, remember me when you come into your kingdom."
>
> Jesus answered him, "I tell you the truth, today you will be with me in paradise." (Luke 23:39–43)

The first criminal was sneering at Jesus, wanting Jesus to prove who He was for his own selfish gain. The second criminal showed he was sorry for his sins by simply saying, "We are getting what our deeds deserve. But this man has done nothing wrong." He believed and repented, and Jesus knew it, promising him paradise. It was too late for the criminal to do any good deeds, as he was in the process of dying, but his true repentance and belief was all that was needed for him to reach eternity in heaven.

This is also our key to eternal life. Jesus gave His life so that we could go to heaven by simply believing it. *"Christ is the end of the law so that there may be righteousness for everyone who believes"* (Romans 10:4). Righteousness can only be obtained through the acceptance of Jesus' blood as the payment for our sins. Once this has happened, we have become God's children. We have then been "born again," having become family members in the household of God (John 3:3–7, Ephesians 2:18–22, and 1 Peter 1:22–2:3).

Once we have become God's children, we are His forever. In the Bible, Jesus sometimes refers to us as sheep, and to Himself as the good shepherd. He said, *"My sheep listen to my voice; I know them, and they follow me. I give them eternal life, and they shall never perish; no one can snatch them out of my hand"* (John 10:27–28). If we get lost, He looks for us until He finds us again (Luke 15:1–7).

As God's children, we have received the gift of the Holy Spirit, the Spirit of sonship. This Spirit testifies that we are God's children and have become heirs of God, and co-heirs with Christ (Romans 8:9–17). *"[We] were included in Christ when [we] heard the word of truth, the gospel of [our] salvation. Having believed, [we] were marked in him with a seal, the promised Holy Spirit, who is a deposit guaranteeing our inheritance until the redemption of those who are God's possession—to the praise of his glory"* (Ephesians 1:13–14).

Many people doubt the permanence of salvation and the promise of eternal Life. They fear that if we sin too much, we will lose our salvation and go to hell after all. The Bible reassures us that because of Jesus' one sacrifice, *"he has made perfect forever those who are being made holy"* (Hebrews 10:14). Therefore, after we have become His children, He has perfected us, even while we are in the process of being made holy. His blood covers us forever. We all still sin, and the Bible tells us that if we claim to be without sin we deceive ourselves, but *"if we confess our sins, he is faithful and just and will forgive us our sins and purify us from all unrighteousness"* (1 John 1:9).

This does not mean that we shouldn't care what we do, deliberately sinning just to take advantage of God's grace. I was once part of a conversation where Christianity was being discussed. There was a man in the group who had broken the hearts of many women, and was quite immoral. He boldly said, "Jesus came for the sinner, not the righteous." It was almost like he was saying, "Jesus came for me, but not for you!" The Bible does say something like this, but what it actually says is, *"For I have not come to call the righteous, but sinners"* (Matthew 9:12–13, emphasis added). This man was actually quite arrogant, almost like he thought he had to keep on sinning or he wouldn't be eligible for God's grace. This is not the case. Perhaps the righteous did not need calling, because they were already part of God's family and didn't need to be added to it. Maybe they were part of the flock that was already safe, and mature enough to be left on their own for awhile while the shepherd went out looking for the lost sheep (Luke 15:3–7).

When Jesus becomes a part of us and lives in our hearts, our desire to sin diminishes—the act of sinning now saddens us and

7

we feel bad when we do it. We no longer have the desire to find out how much we can get away with, but rather we are filled with the Holy Spirit, who gives us the desire to please our Lord and bring others to Him. We are now dead to sin, but alive in Christ, and we are strongly discouraged from deliberately sinning (Romans 6 and Hebrews 10:26–29). Our true belief in Jesus will help us live right and keep us from continuing in sin (1 John 3:1–10).

What about someone who claims to be a Christian but doesn't show forth any good works and doesn't bear good fruit? People are often quick to judge others because of their deeds. The unbelieving world seems to know exactly what Christians should or shouldn't do, and uses the shortcomings of others as an excuse to keep rejecting the Lord in their own lives. Even older, mature Christians fall into the trap of stepping on little brothers and sisters instead of bearing with them or teaching them. When someone becomes a newborn Christian, they are like the newborn baby who needs to grow up (1 Corinthians 3:1–3 and 1 Peter 2:1–3).

This process doesn't happen overnight. In fact, we never really "arrive" in the works department. If we think we've made it, we are probably filled with pride and self-righteousness. When an unbeliever comes to us tattling and gloating about what they saw some Christian doing, tell them about the grace and mercy of Jesus, who loves us despite our weaknesses. Tell them that we are Christians because of what Jesus has done for us, not because of our deeds.

Our sinful nature and spirit will keep on battling as long as we live. Paul had this kind of struggle, too. In his inner being he delighted in God's law, but his body didn't always do as he desired in his spirit (Romans 7:14–25). Paul looked forward to Jesus rescuing him from this body of death, and so can we. Only God knows the real truth about someone, since He knows the heart.

Romans 14 talks about weak and strong people, and tells us, *"Who are you to judge someone else's servant?"* (Romans 14:4) Perhaps the dim light of an immature believer shines quite brightly in a much darker section of the world than ours. The struggling believer needs us to pray for and help him. The Bible tells us to *"preach the Word: be prepared in season and out of season; correct, rebuke, and encourage—with great patience and careful instruction"* (2 Timothy 4:2). When we feel God leading us to rebuke or correct someone, we need to be careful not to discourage him, lest he give up trying. When we are faithful to do our part, God's kingdom will grow, despite our human flaws.

Many doubters of secure salvation in Jesus Christ quote Matthew 7:21–23, which says, *"Not everyone who says to me 'Lord, Lord,' will enter the kingdom of heaven, but only he who does the will of my Father who is in heaven. Many will say to me on that day, 'Lord, Lord, did we not prophesy in your name, and in your name drive out demons and perform many miracles? Then I will tell them plainly, 'I never knew you. Away from me, you evildoers!'"* This is, indeed, a sobering thought, one that makes us wonder what Jesus meant. It sounds as if those people were depending on their good works to get to heaven, not on Jesus' saving grace. Jesus never knew them, so maybe they never received Him as Saviour and Lord. Perhaps they drove demons out of people who didn't have demons to begin with.

What does it mean to do God's will? Jesus talks about this in John 6:40, saying, *"For my Father's will is that everyone who looks to the Son and believes in him shall have eternal life, and I will raise him up at the last day."* This again reinforces the fact that belief in Jesus is our key to eternal life. This belief usually shows itself in love to others, bearing good fruit through doing good deeds. The important thing is that the works we do are built on the foundation of Jesus Christ. The Bible tells us that our work will be shown for what it is. If what we have built survives, we will receive a reward, but if our work is burned up, we will suffer loss; although we will still be saved, it will be as one escaping through the flames (see 1 Corinthians 3:11–15).

The truly righteous will have forgotten about their good works by the time they get to heaven.

> Then the King will say to those on his right, "Come, you who are blessed by my Father; take your inheritance, the kingdom prepared for you since the creation of the world. For I was hungry and you gave me something to eat, I was thirsty and you gave me something to drink, I was a stranger and you invited me in, I needed clothes and you clothed me, I was sick and you looked after me, I was in prison and you came to visit me."
>
> Then the righteous will answer him, "Lord, when did we see you hungry and feed you, or thirsty and give you something to drink? When did we see you a stranger and invite you in, or needing clothes and clothe you? When did we see you sick or in prison and go to visit you?"
>
> The King will reply, "I tell you the truth, whatever you did for one of the least of these brothers of mine, you did for me." (Matthew 25:34–40)

Good works are often a natural way of life to believers. If they see a need and they have the ability to meet that need, they do it, and it's not a big deal to them. But Jesus won't forget. He will reward believers for all the good things they did which they never got thanked for (see Matthew 6:1–4, 10:42).

If you are reading this today, and you aren't sure that God is your Father, I want to give you the opportunity to become his child right now. I became a believer when I was fifteen, after I finished reading Arthur S. Maxwell's *The Bible Story* series. There was an invitation at the back of Volume 10, and I committed my life to Jesus after reading it.

Pray with me.

> Lord Jesus, I don't know you, but I have been told that this desire to learn about you comes from your Spirit inviting and enabling me to come to you. Please forgive my sins, and come live in my heart. Lord, I am scared of death and I ask you to give me your peace. Help me to be your child, and teach me your ways. Thank you, Lord Jesus, for dying for my sins, giving me salvation, and promising me eternal life. Amen.

Welcome to God's family! If you prayed this prayer (or a similar one) in your heart, you are now officially a child of God. You now have the Holy Spirit living in your heart, and He will be with you always. He will never leave you or forsake you, and you can look forward to being with Jesus for all eternity to come. Praise God!

CHAPTER TWO

JUST AS I... AM?

"DAD, GIVE ME MY SHARE OF THE ESTATE," DEMANDED Earl. "It will be mine someday anyway, and I need the money now!"

The nerve! Can you imagine what Earl's dad must have felt like, knowing that his beloved son couldn't wait until he died to get the material gain he envisioned? If Earl had been one of your children, you probably would have scolded him severely and possibly taken away the allowance he was already getting in order for him to learn to appreciate what he had.

Earl's dad, however, did exactly what Earl asked of him. He sold part of his property and gave Earl his share of the estate. Earl left home a few weeks later and moved to a distant town where his friend from school had moved three years earlier. It didn't take him long to make more friends, and he had a blast. His friends were more than willing to participate in whatever Earl decided to do, as long as he paid the bill.

It wasn't long before the money was gone. Earl's friends left as quickly as they had come, and Earl was left alone and homeless. To top it all off, a vast area of the country experienced drought that year, drying up the crops and causing severe fam-ine in the land. In time, Earl found a job working for a local hog farmer. It didn't pay well, but it provided a shelter for him to sleep and some spending money. He often went hungry, though, as food was scarce and prices were exceedingly high. Sometimes he longed to eat the pig's food, just to be filled for once.

Earl often thought of his dad and older brother, and missed them terribly. However, thought of going back filled him with shame and remorse. He was an adult now, and Dad was no longer responsible to provide for his needs. It wasn't his dad's fault that he had been so foolish and squandered away his in-heritance. He wasn't about to go back and be a burden to him now.

One day, Earl had a brainwave. He remembered how the servants on his dad's farm always had enough to eat and a cozy little house to live in. Perhaps he could go back and be a servant on his dad's farm. With this thought in mind, Earl said goodbye to the farmer and his family and started the long journey home. He traveled for many days, stopping to rest only when he be-came too weary to go on. As he traveled further south, more green lined the roads, giving evidence of sufficient rainfall in the area. He was now able to satisfy the growling of his empty stomach with wild berries and other natural plants growing be-side the path.

Finally, about two weeks later, he caught a glimpse of his dad's farm in the distance. He started running towards home until a thought suddenly struck him: *What if I'm not welcome?* He knew only too well that he did not deserve his dad's love after being so selfish and rude. He slowed down to a snail's pace and kept on towards home.

Earl was so engrossed in his thoughts, his eyes dejectedly focused on the ground in front of him, that he failed to see a figure approaching him in the distance. Suddenly, he heard running footsteps coming towards him. He looked up just in time to catch a glimpse of his dad's outstretched arms before he was engulfed by his warm embrace. He could feel his dad's tears on his cheek as he kept saying, "My son, you're alive! You're safe! I'm so glad you came home!"

"Dad, I'm very ashamed of what I've done. I'm no longer worthy to be your son. Can I come and be your servant?"

But Dad wasn't listening. He was already giving orders to the servants who had followed him. "Quick! Get him some fresh clothes to wear. Find some nice shoes to put on his feet. Bring the best cow on the farm and kill it. Invite all our friends and neighbours. Let's have a feast and celebrate, for my son has come home!"

So they began to celebrate. Earl, dirty and smelly from travel dust and hog farm odour, had no time to bathe or get a word in edgewise as he was swept into the joyous celebration.

This is a similar story to the one in the Bible often referred to as "The Prodigal Son" (Luke 15:11–32). Jesus used this story to illustrate God's love for us as repentant sinners, God being the Father in the story. He said there is great rejoicing in heaven and among the angels of God whenever a sinner repents (Luke 15:7–10). The Father in the story of the prodigal son had obviously been keeping a hopeful lookout for his son's return, and ran to meet him when he saw him coming in the distance. He immediately called for a feast of rejoicing to celebrate his son's safe return.

But the older brother became angry. He had never left home, and was a loyal companion to his dad, helping him on the family farm and giving up his own personal ambitions. On this particular day, he had been extremely busy in the fields. He was tired, his feet ached, and he couldn't wait to eat and get to bed extra early. It is no wonder that the sound of music and the smell of beef on the barbeque irritated him. When he found out the cause of the celebration, he became angrier still and shouted at his dad, *"Look! All these years I've been slaving for you and never disobeyed your orders. Yet you never gave me even a young goat so that I could celebrate with my friends. But when this son of yours who has squandered your property with prostitutes comes home, you kill the fattened calf for him!"* (Luke 15:29–30)

Did the older brother have a right to be angry? If we had been in his shoes, we probably would have reacted the same way. Our human logic and wisdom would have said, "That's not fair!" Our reaction would probably have been to punish our brother, tell him "I told you so," make him pay some kind of penance to show his true repentance, and then hesitantly accept him back into the family if he promised to be good. The question is, did Jesus tell us this story in order for us to follow the example of the Father who represents God, or the older brother who possibly represents older brothers in the church?

The Bible tells us that "God is love," that we are to love as He loved and forgive our brother from the heart (see 1 John 4:7–11, John 13:34–35, and Matthew 18:35). I believe we need to follow the Father's example, not the brother's. We should be welcoming and forgiving, extending God's grace to others. In fact, there are serious consequences for those who refuse to extend God's grace and forgiveness to others when they themselves have received His mercy (see Matthew 18:21–35).

What might have happened if the Father in the story had gone out for the day, and the older brother had been the first to welcome his lost brother home? We can almost hear the older brother lash out in anger and resentment, even putting road-blocks in the way of his brother ever reuniting with his Father. He might have said something like, "How dare you show your face here after hurting Dad like you did! You should be ashamed! I really don't think Dad wants to see you. Who knows what kind of diseases you carry from whatever scum you've been with! Why don't you go and clean up your life, get your act together, earn some money, and then come back and show Dad that you aren't a total loser after all?" We can almost see the de-jected young man turn away and trudge back the way he came without ever reaching his Dad's embrace. We can see him give up on life and commit suicide, thinking that there is no hope for him, while the Father keeps scanning the horizon, praying for his son's return.

We sometimes dare to invite our unbelieving family mem-bers, friends, and neighbours to revival meetings and church events, hoping and praying that they will accept the altar call at the end of the service and become Christians. We sing the hymn "Just as I Am," reassuring them that God loves them and will accept them just the way they are.

In many churches, however, this is where acceptance by men is different than acceptance by God. Even though God truly does accept repentant sinners immediately, people often don't. This is usually when older brothers step in and insist that new believers prove themselves first before being accepted into the congregation. When new believers show interest in officially becoming members of the local church, they are given a list of

17

rules to follow, standards to live up to, classes to attend, and in some cases a dress code to follow before they are fit for acceptance in the congregation. It is like following the older brother's example of not wanting to share the Father's love until sufficient restitution is made. Many encourage new Christians to prove their faith first by doing good works and completely changing their habits and lifestyle. In fact, it is often the good works that are promoted rather than the heart change that happens when Christ enters a person's life. Perfection has to be portrayed, at least by outward appearances.

The fact is, none of us can earn favour with God by working for Him. Salvation was given to us as a free gift as a result of Christ's death on the cross in our place. The Bible says, *"For it is by grace you have been saved, through faith—and this not from yourselves, it is the gift of God—not by works, so that no one can boast"* (Ephesians 2:8–9) We haven't earned our salvation by being faithful church members for many years. The new believer coming into our midst is just as worthy of the Father's love as we are. In fact, we are all unworthy of His awesome grace, love, and forgiveness. When we, as mature and older brothers and sisters in Christ, make up all kinds of rules and conditions for other people to adhere to before we accept them, we are just like the Pharisees and teachers of the Law to whom Jesus said, *"Woe to you, teachers of the law and Pharisees, you hypocrites! You shut the kingdom of heaven in men's faces. You yourselves do not enter, nor will you let those enter who are trying to"* (Matthew 23:13).

In the early church, repentance from sin and belief in the good news of Jesus' death on the cross was all that was needed for baptism, which turned a believer into a member of the universal Church of God. Peter preached repentance and baptism for the forgiveness of sins in the name of Jesus Christ. Those who accepted his message were baptized, and about three thousand were added to their number that day. They continued praising God, and the Lord added to their number daily those who were being saved (see Acts 2:36–47).

When Paul and Silas were released from prison by God sending an earthquake, the jailer was about to commit suicide, thinking that his prisoners had escaped.

> But Paul shouted, "Don't harm yourself! We are all here!"
>
> The jailer called for lights, rushed in and fell trembling before Paul and Silas. He then brought them out and asked, "Sirs, what must I do to be saved?"
>
> They replied, "Believe in the Lord Jesus, and you will be saved—you and your household." Then they spoke the word of the Lord to him and all the others in his house.
>
> At that hour of the night the jailer took them and washed their wounds; then immediately he and all his family were baptized. (Acts 16:28–33).

The disciples (or apostles) were being obedient to the commission given them by Jesus after He arose and before He ascended into heaven. He had told them to go and make disciples of all nations, baptizing them in the name of the Father, Son, and Holy Spirit, and teaching them to obey what Jesus commanded (Matthew 28:19 and Mark 16:15; also see Acts 1:8–9).

Many churches today have lost or added to this commission given by our Lord. Manmade traditions have replaced belief in

Jesus and His finished work on the cross as a means by which to become a church member.

Jesus said, *"I am the way and the truth and the life. No one comes to the Father except through me"* (John 14:6). Through Jesus, we can come to our Father and be embraced by His loving arms, welcomed back as was the prodigal son.

As we go forth making disciples, let's remember to follow the Father's example of love and acceptance. Let us not be like the jealous older brother and force our younger brothers and sisters to grow and mature first in order to be accepted into the congregation. We who plant or water a seed in order to make disciples are only servants through whom others come to believe. It is God who makes them grow, and He will cause new believers to change and grow and give them gifts as He desires (see 1 Corinthians 3:5–7, 12:11).

It is not our job to change people by force. When God causes change, it is done by the Holy Spirit from the inside out, and it is much more effective than when older brothers bully change forcefully. Enforcement of the Law often encourages people to live with a mask on, not daring to show their weaknesses or ask for help for fear of being judged by men. The result is many congregations filled with people who put on the face that people want to see, while inwardly they are struggling. It stunts the positive growth of new and more mature believers.

A few years ago, our family moved to a new town where we didn't know anybody. When we started attending one of the local churches, we found it to be much different from the church back home. What kept us coming back again and again was the love of Christ within the congregation. The issue of becoming an official member of that denomination never came up, until we asked questions about it. They automatically considered people to be members after regularly attending for three months, and valued their input and ideas. Their motto seemed to be, "You believe in Jesus? Welcome, brother!" We were accepted as family, just as we were. They watered the seed that was already planted in our hearts and allowed God to work with what needed changing and healing in our lives. We will forever be grateful to St. Andrew's and Peter Dyck, the pastor there, for being obedient disciples of Jesus Christ, following His example of love and acceptance while providing valuable, life-changing biblical teaching at the same time. The Bible became alive for us and we grew spiritually as never before.

It is easy to see, though, why churches struggle in this area of accepting others into their midst. Christian leaders are called to lead the flock and will be held accountable before God (Ezekiel 34, Hebrews 13:17, and 1 Peter 5:2–3). Many feel that the way to lead is to make sure that people prove themselves first; then, if they are indeed worthy, they can become church members. It is no wonder that the free gift of salvation to undeserving sinners is unfathomable, even to many believers. If we study the above scriptures, we see that leaders are called to live as an example to the flock. They are not to rule over them harshly, but rather care for them, binding up the injured, helping the weak, and seeking the lost. I believe that God is much more concerned about people not getting the message about Jesus and the love of God than He is that all church members portray perfection in order to be part of the church.

It is vital, though, that the members of Christ's body be true believers. The Bible tells us not to be yoked with unbelievers, for righteousness and wickedness have nothing in common (2 Corinthians 6:14–16). It is therefore important that the people who vote and make decisions within God's Church be Believers, ensuring that decisions made within the body of Christ are led by the Lord.

In the early Church, they counted the new believers who were being added to their number, and somehow kept a record of paperwork. Today, most churches have a much more complex way of adding members to their congregation. When manmade traditions are the basis for acceptance within Christ's Church, it is easy for people to put on the acceptable outward apparel and say the expected words in order to become part of the church for other reasons than to promote Christ.

For example, a couple wants to get married and the only politically correct way to accomplish this is to join the church first. After a few generations of this, churches become filled with people who follow expected traditions but know very little about the Lord or His Word, the Bible. Personally, I think it's wonderful when couples do become part of a church family before they get married, so that they have a congregation of people to pray for them in their new life together. However, baptism and church membership are not marriage requirements! Many religious Christians do not condone non-church weddings, and their strong legalistic convictions encourage others to join the church in order to keep peace within the family, even when they neither believe nor have faith in Christ.

I remember thinking about joining a church after I started dating. I wondered which church my boyfriend and I would join, should we decide to get married. Even though I had read my Bible quite a bit, my thoughts about joining a church had nothing to do with following Jesus. Thankfully, by the time I got baptized and became a church member, I had first become a believer. Sometimes the classes taught by churches to people contemplating baptism and/or church membership are good tools for turning a small interest in Christ into a lifelong faith.

Churches who profess Jesus Christ as Lord need to follow His example of loving sinners, teaching the truth from God's Word, and welcoming new believers into their midst. When the Gospel is preached and people become believers, they can be baptized and welcomed into God's family immediately, just like in the early Church. While it is necessary to ensure that decisions within the Body of Christ are made by believers, it should never be harder to become a member in a church than it is to become a Christian.

The sharing of a personal testimony and confession of Jesus Christ as Lord and Saviour by new believers is an awesome way of them being welcomed into the church. The Bible encourages us to acknowledge Jesus Christ before men, and Jesus promises that if we do, He will also acknowledge us before God (Matthew 10:32; also see Romans 10:9–10 and 1 Corinthians 12:3). Asking new believers to testify about what Christ has done for them lets them know that other believers care and want to hear about their experience. It also confirms to the existing church body that these people are, indeed, believers—and not false teachers or imposters. This helps to prevent people from joining a church for the wrong reasons. A simple confession of faith in Jesus as Lord should be sufficient evidence for older brothers and church leadership to have no qualms about welcoming new believers into their congregation with open arms.

Sometimes people have joined churches without becoming believers first. Sadly, they could end up lost for eternity because they thought they did what they needed to do in order to be saved, and everyone else assumed they were Christians because they joined the church.

Responsible leaders are encouraged when believers openly confess Christ as Lord during the membership process (or at any other time). It gives them peace of mind, knowing where the person stands, and that he or she can be trusted to further the work of the Lord within the church, promoting the love of Christ within the community. Fellow believers can rejoice about having a new "saint" within the family, and then concentrate their efforts on finding others who might still be lost (Luke 15).

Jesus is not willing that anybody should perish. Rather, He wants everyone to come to repentance (2 Peter 3:9). He longs to gather people together as a hen gathers her chicks under her wings, but people are often unwilling (Matthew 23:37). Religion often does a better job of pushing people away, rather than drawing them to Christ.

We as human beings are strange creatures. Often the harder something is to obtain, the more popular and sought after it becomes. We can buy a Co-op membership so that we can later collect dividends or become shareholders in other companies. We can join a sports team, buy a gym membership, or join the cycling club, all for a fee. Nothing in life is free. Jesus gave his life as a ransom to pardon us from our sins and give us eternal life (Mark 10:45). People can't fathom or accept this free gift of salvation, so they have added their own "fee" — or list of works you have to accomplish in order to be accepted as a Christian within certain groups and denominations. The more hoops people have to jump through in order to be part of a group, the more popular it is and the faster it grows. The more rules there are to follow, the more people can show off how good they have become. The more "separate" the group, the holier they can look at a distance.

An acquaintance of mine who had separated from her husband once said, "I find it much easier to live a Christian life now that I am on my own." I believe her. She doesn't have to get along with anybody but herself. She doesn't have to serve anyone unless she feels like it. While it might be easier to live as a hermit, it doesn't fulfill Jesus' commission. It doesn't promote going out into the world and bringing in the lost. In a healthy, growing, Bible-based Church, there should be some unbelievers who come to check out the Gospel because someone from that congregation was a witness of Christ's love to them. There should be a few newborn believers who still mess up because they are just starting to learn how to follow Christ. There should be a few toddlers who are walking, but still stumble and fall as they learn. There should be mature believers who clean up the messes and help up the fallen, encouraging them to try again and not give up. There should be some people leaving as God calls them to evangelize elsewhere in the world.

The focus of such a church should be on outreach, evangelism, and discipleship rather than enlarging the local numbers and portraying perfection. Being part of the body of Christ requires us to bear with others and get along with them. It involves serving others, even when we don't feel like it. It is about more than just getting along with ourselves; it's about going the extra mile and bringing others in, because Jesus is not willing that any should be lost.

Let us as Christians today welcome people when they show interest in Jesus, and let us not hinder them from coming to Him because of our current traditions. Let's make sure that when we lead someone to the Lord and he or she converts to the Christian faith, they will have the true Gospel to share with others—the gospel of salvation and grace to undeserving sinners who have done nothing to earn it. They have simply repented from their sin and put their faith in Jesus Christ as Saviour and Lord. Perhaps if Christians within churches follow the Father's example of love to repentant sinners, many more will come to Christ and be saved. Perhaps thousands could be added to our number in a single day, just like in the early Church.

Let us not cheapen the free gift of Jesus' sacrifice on our behalf by making His body, the Church, just another club to join. Jesus is in the process of gathering to Himself as many as possible who are willing to come. Let us not hinder them, but welcome them and rejoice along with the angels every time a lost soul comes to Him and is saved.

Just as I am—without one plea,
But that Thy blood was shed for me,
And that Thou bidst me come to Thee,
O Lamb of God, I come

Just as I am—and waiting not
To rid my soul of one dark blot,
To Thee, whose blood can cleanse each spot,
O Lamb of God, I come!

—"Just as I Am," by Charlotte Elliott
and William B. Bradbury (1835)

CHAPTER THREE

WHICH CHURCH IS THE RIGHT ONE FOR ME?

"WELL, I GUESS WE JUST WON'T 'DO' CHURCH," TRACY sighed, throwing up her hands in exasperation. "There is no way we can please both your parents and mine, no matter what we do!"

"I'm with you," agreed Bob, her fiancé. "Although I did always enjoy being part of the Christmas pageants as a child."

"I enjoyed the special things, too," lamented Tracy, "but for the most part, church was a timeout, sitting quietly trying not to squirm as the preacher talked on and on about things I couldn't understand."

"I thought it might work out for us and please our parents if we went to a totally different church," said Bob. "But when we tried that new church on River Drive the other day, they passed around the offering basket three times, and I felt really bad not putting anything in it the second two times. I really don't think we can afford to go there, especially right now with the wedding expenses and starting our own home. You know, all we really want is a wedding, and you're right, half our family won't be happy if we join the other church. All I see is one big problem—

unless we just hire a Justice of the Peace, rent the community hall, and keep it simple. At least then if trouble starts, it will stay in the family. Can you imagine what might happen if the wedding was at my church, and your mom and my Auntie Jill started a discussion about church differences?"

"We would have absolute chaos in a matter of minutes," agreed Tracy. "It could easily turn into the most heated debate of the century, and that would ruin our wedding day."

Tracy and Bob did stand by their decision and had a small simple wedding at the Legion Hall, officiated by a Justice of the Peace. Their parents were somewhat disappointed, but thought it just as well, since the wedding couldn't be at their own church anyway. It was better to have worldly children than to risk losing them to another denomination.

Bob and Tracy's problem is not a new one. Most of us have either faced the same dilemma or know others who have gone through it. How do people find the right church for themselves? Is any particular denomination superior to the others? Which church is the most biblically accurate? Most of us have heard people promoting their own denomination, even though many of them have never visited other congregations.

When I was a little girl, my favourite brand of truck was Chevrolet, and the best tractor was International. Why? It wasn't like I knew anything about either of them. Chevy trucks and International tractors just had to be the best, because my dad owned them! Sometimes my little friends and I had heated discussions about this and got mad at one another because their dads owned different models than my Dad, and they couldn't both be the best.

What does this have to do with church? Well, in Paul's day, people literally had arguments similar to this, except they argued about which leader they were following, bragging about their own leader and promoting him above the others. Some said they followed Paul. Others said they followed Apollos, Cephas, or Christ. Since Paul had been promoting Christ—and Christ only—he got really frustrated and asked, *"Is Christ divided? Was Paul crucified for you? Were you baptized into the name of Paul?"* (1 Corinthians 1:13) He was thankful that he hadn't physically baptized most of them. He said that their quarrelling meant that they were mere infants in Christ, and worldly. He pointed out that all of these men, besides Christ, were only servants through whom others came to believe. He explained how one person can plant a seed, another person can water it, but that it is God who makes it grow (see 1 Corinthians 1:11–15, 3:1–11).

Today, people proudly say things like: "I'm Mennonite." "I'm Catholic." "I'm Pentecostal." "I'm Lutheran." "I'm Anglican." "I'm an E-FREE member." "I belong to the Reform Church." Rarely will anyone simply say, "I'm a Christian and I follow Christ." Jesus is the Head of the Church and should be the most important focus of our Christian life (Ephesians 1:22).

Parents often stress the importance of staying true to what has been taught, implying that their children must continue in the same faith/denomination/tradition as their ancestors. Unfortunately, when two people from two different denominations fall in love and want to get married, they can't both stay a member within their own congregation and become one in marriage at the same time. Some have tried it, but it usually results in unnecessary struggles within the home. It is therefore important to realize where this teaching comes from, and what it really says.

This saying is actually biblical, in part, and only slightly misquoted. It is found in a letter written by Paul to his younger brother in Christ, Timothy. He encourages Timothy by saying, *"But as for you, continue in what you have learned and have become convinced of, because you know those from whom you learned it, and how from infancy you have known the holy Scriptures, which are able to make you wise for salvation through faith in Christ Jesus"* (2 Timothy 3:14–15). Paul did not encourage Timothy to hold onto the traditions of his ancestors. Timothy had been taught the truth from Scripture since childhood, and this is what Paul encouraged him to continue in. Timothy's knowledge of Scripture would make him wise for salvation through faith in Christ Jesus.

This is our key to finding the right church for ourselves. Salvation comes only through faith in Jesus Christ and His finished work on the cross. Any church or denomination that teaches this vital truth is part of God's universal Church. The Bible teaches that all believers are brothers and sisters in Jesus Christ. Therefore, all of us who have been baptized into Christ have clothed ourselves with Christ. It doesn't matter if we are Jew, Greek, slave, free, male, female, barbarian, circumcised, or uncircumcised… in Christ, we are one family (see Galatians 3:26–29, Colossians 3:11, and 1 Corinthians 12:12–27).

The body of Christ consists of many parts, and each one is essential to the functioning of the universal Church. Just like individual people perform different duties and purposes within the local church, different groups of believers draw different types of people to God's saving grace, using various different methods, languages, and cultural traditions. Let's face it, most of us value our upbringing and the faith we were taught as a child, even if it was lacking in biblical knowledge and focused mostly on cultural traditions.

Traditions kind of get passed onto our children just because they've always seen us do things a certain way. Many times, traditions were born out of convenience and became habit because they were easy to do. Many traditions have no biblical instruction supporting them, but they are also not forbidden, so it basically boils down to personal preferences. The only thing is, as Spirit-filled Believers, if we are stuck on traditions and things getting done a specific way, the work of the Holy Spirit is often hindered, because the vessel is unwilling to act in freedom to the inspiration of the Holy Spirit's spontaneous guidance within us.

My first language was Low German, a dialect which until recently had no written form. My parents belonged to a German church which spoke the official High German language, which was never spoken at home. I started worshipping God by playing church, singing songs with my playmates and imitating our parents as we made up words that probably didn't exist. Even then, the Holy Spirit touched me and gave me a desire to worship in a language I couldn't speak. My parents started attending a different church when I was fifteen, and this is when I first heard the Gospel preached in a language I could understand. It was here that I became a Christian, got baptized, and married the man I loved. Circumstances caused us to move elsewhere for work, and we worshipped with a totally different denomination for about a year. However, this church was quite a distance from where we lived, so we started attending still a different church service with still a different denomination within the local community.

Through all of this, God kept leading, guiding, and growing us. He used many different servants within the body of Christ to draw us ever closer to Himself. When we moved back to our hometown several years later, our Morinville Church family prayed over us and sent us on our way as missionaries of Christ to another place. They firmly believed and taught that all believers are missionaries within the perimeter of their own lives as they interact with others. In fact, we were often encouraged and commissioned week by week to be vessels of God's love, especially in our own homes, schools, and workplaces—in fact, anywhere within the local community.

The Bible teaches this same important truth. We are commissioned to go into the world, making disciples of all nations, baptizing them in the name of the Father, Son, and Holy Spirit and teaching them everything Christ commanded (Matthew 28:19–20). This mission is not limited to a few designated foreign missionaries and Church leadership. It applies to all baptized believers who have become disciples through this ongoing process, as each one is called to keep promoting the Gospel. "The world" includes where we currently live. There is no part of God's earth excluded from the need for ministry and evangelism. There are, of course, different gifts and abilities within different people, so we have different ways of showing God's love to others. Some speak boldly, while others quietly smile and encourage or help out where they are able. The important thing is that we use the gifts and talents God has given us to promote His love in our world (1 Corinthians 12–14).

This is really what church is about. As we grow and continue in our faith, others will be drawn to God's saving grace through us. This is the mission of the church.

If our Morinville Church family had been selfish and concerned only about themselves, they might have taught us that they were the only "right" church, and kept us there. This would have kept our offering money within their local church treasury, and kept our talents and gifts at work amongst themselves. It is what many cults promote. Instead, our church family recognized God's hand at work in our lives and considered it a privilege to commission us onward to where God was leading us.

But shouldn't we be concerned about cults? Doesn't the Bible warn us about false prophets leading people astray? (see 2 Corinthians 11, 2 Peter 2, 1 John 4:1–6, and Jude 4–19) Don't parents have a right to desire that their children and grandchildren belong to the same congregation as themselves? Of course, as parents our natural instincts are to protect our children and keep them safe. Instinct tells us that the best way to do this is to keep them as close to us as possible. However, we have already discovered that we can't always be there. The best way to protect our children is to entrust them to God's custody. We also need to teach them the truth, that Jesus Christ is Lord and is the one we are loyal to.

Another truth is the fact that God's Church is universal and includes all believers everywhere. If someone is teaching that their one particular congregation or denomination is the only right church, it is probably teaching other false doctrines as well. It is a good idea to check your own Bible to make sure that what is being taught is actual truth from God's Word. If children know the love of Jesus and have been taught the truth from Scripture since childhood, the way Timothy was, they will be able to know the difference between the truth and lies. This will protect them from cults and false prophets. This will also promote the truth from God's Word and the love of Christ that we have taught them to spread wherever they go, thus fulfilling Jesus' commission.

Just a few short years ago, my husband and I were in Bob and Tracy's shoes. We had to choose a church for ourselves, knowing that if we made the decision we eventually did make, my husband's family might not come to our wedding. As it turned out, they did come and we cried tears of joy when we saw they had. Some of our friends weren't as fortunate. They got married with half the family missing because they belonged to a church which encouraged denominational loyalty to the point that members did not feel free to visit other congregations.

Don't get me wrong, it is a good thing to be loyal to your church and a dependable member of your congregation. We just need to recognize that other churches are part of God's family, too. We aren't the only ones.

Jesus' disciple John came to Him one day:

> "Teacher," said John, "we saw a man driving out demons in your name and we told him to stop, because he was not one of us."
>
> "Do not stop him," Jesus said. "No one who does a miracle in my name can in the next moment say anything bad about me, for whoever is not against us is for us." (Mark 9:38–40; see also Matthew 12:30)

Paul also realized that some people preached Christ for the wrong reasons, out of envy and selfish ambition. Others preached Christ out of love and goodwill. Paul was in prison at the time and could do little to rectify the situation. He said, *"But what does it matter? The important thing is that in every way, whether from false motives or true, Christ is preached. And because of this I rejoice"* (Philippians 1:18).

We can also rejoice that Christ is preached, even though imperfect people possibly preach for the wrong reasons. God is magnificent and works through us to draw others to Himself, despite our human weaknesses. God's family consists of all believers in the world who proclaim Jesus Christ as Lord. It is wonderful to be part of God's family, knowing that we have brothers and sisters all around the world.

Remember that there are only two teams in this world. We are either for Christ, or against Him. When we are for Christ, He will use us as vessels of love to bring others to himself, no matter which congregation we are part of.

CHAPTER FOUR

WHICH BIBLE IS THE RIGHT ONE?

JACK STARED AT THE BOOK IN MY HANDS WITH disbelief. "You read the NIV Bible! Cousin Joe's uncle said there are missing verses in that Bible. The only Bible I now trust is the King James that I grew up with."

The encouraging visit with Cousin Jack and his wife Stella came to an abrupt halt. The beautiful scriptures we had just enjoyed together now seemed disgraced. It was as if anything I might say would be unbelievable anyway, since I was influenced by a different version of the Bible.

The truth? We didn't know if what they said was true. I checked the reference they gave me, and sure enough the verse was missing from the passage and added at the bottom of the page instead. Were the missing verses in the NIV Bible deliberately left out, or did someone add verses to other translations?

I had grown to love the modern-day English of the NIV Bible and was compelled to research various Bible origins and get to the truth of the matter. My research involved reading the preface of various Bibles and searching the encyclopedia and internet. I was astonished when the encyclopedia pointed out that the discovery of ancient biblical manuscripts in the nineteenth century led to the realization of how many errors and deliberate changes had been made in the copying and recopying of manuscripts.

So which translation is accurate? I was amazed to discover that the Bible has been translated into 1,118 languages and dialects. Some portions have been published in over 1,300 languages. The Roman Catholic Old Testament contains additional material that is not in the Hebrew Scriptures. In Protestant Bibles, such material is called the Apocrypha, and is either left out or printed as an appendix to the Old Testament.

After the invention of the printing press in the fifteenth century, the Vulgate was printed for the first time. It was called the Gutenberg Bible, and became the official Bible of the Roman Catholic Church in 1546.

William Tyndale, a Protestant inspired by Luther and using original texts, published an important English translation of the New Testament in 1525, and of the Pentateuch (the first five books of the Old Testament collectively ascribed to Moses) in 1530. Tyndale's work was a major source for Miles Coverdale's complete English Bible in 1535. The revised work of both men became the basis for the Great Bible in 1539.

The Great Bible was edited by Coverdale and printed by order of King Henry VIII to replace the Vulgate in England. English Protestants in Geneva, Switzerland produced the Geneva Bible, based on Tyndale's Bible, which was influenced by Calvin.

By this time, Catholics had begun to translate the Vulgate into English. The result, The Dovay Bible, was the work of a group of English Catholic scholars from 1582–1610. It became the official English version of the Catholic Scriptures and was later revised by Bishop Richard Challoner.

The Authorized King James Version of the Bible is based on Tyndale's translation and original texts. It was produced in 1611 by six groups of churchmen at the command of King James I. A newer revised version of the King James Bible was published in England in 1881 and 1885. The New King James Version was published in Nashville, Tennessee in 1982. Therefore, there are three different translations of King James Bibles—the Authorized, the Revised, and the New King James.

The New International Version (NIV) Bible is a completely new translation of the Holy Bible made by over a hundred scholars working directly from the best available Hebrew, Aramaic, and Greek texts. Participants came from the United States, Great Britain, Canada, Australia, and New Zealand. They were from many different denominations, including Anglican, Assemblies of God, Baptist, Brethren, Christian Reformed, Church of Christ, Evangelical Free, Lutheran, Mennonite, Methodist, Nazarene, Presbyterian, Wesleyan, and others. This diversity helped to safeguard this translation from sectarian bias. The first printing of the entire NIV Bible was completed in 1978.

As we can see, there are many different translations of the Holy Bible in one language, and it has been translated into more than a thousand different languages and dialects. How can we tell if our translation might have been tampered with? We have several choices:

1. We can learn to read and understand Hebrew, Aramaic, and Greek and study God's Word in as original a translation as possible.

2. We have the option of cross-referencing the Bible translations available to us. We can

also use a dictionary, thesaurus, concordance, commentary, or other books to help us better understand what we read. We can find these kinds of resources at the library, Christian bookstore, or church.

3. We can trust the Holy Spirit to reveal to us the truth in Scripture, no matter in which version we read it.

I remember being frustrated when people would come to my door and share Scripture with me. If I understood something differently than they did, they would say, "Oh, but that means something else in the Greek." Many scholars disagree. The Bible says that "*all Scripture is God-breathed and is useful for teaching, rebuking, correcting and training in righteousness, so that the man of God may be thoroughly equipped for every good work*" (2 Timothy 3:16–17, emphasis added).

If all Scripture is God-breathed, then we can trust that God did, in fact, inspire the original writers, and He also inspired the translators who learned more than one language in order to bring us God's Word in our own tongue. We can trust that the words we are reading when we study our Bible are the words that God wants us to apply to ourselves for today, as He feeds us spiritually through His Word. We do not have to worry when we read "*God is love*" (1 John 4:8) that it might be translated wrong, and therefore not true. We can rest assured when we read this passage that God is love, that He loves us, and that He wants us to live in love.

God is the creator of all languages. He stopped the building of the Tower of Babel by giving the builders many languages, causing them to scatter over the whole earth (Genesis 11:1–9). Since God gave us many languages, we cannot presume that any one language is better than the others. In fact, when the Holy Spirit was given to the first disciples at Pentecost, they spoke in many different languages so that all the people from many nations heard the Gospel in their own tongue! (Acts 2) Many were saved that first Pentecost as they believed the message they heard and were baptized upon their faith.

Sometimes controlling leaders really don't want people to read and understand God's Word for themselves. It causes them to lose control, especially if they have been teaching false doctrine rather than truth from the Bible. When God gave the gift of tongues to the first apostles so that all the listeners could understand the Gospel message, He clearly showed us that He wanted all men to understand!

Some fear that translating the Bible into other languages causes some content to be added and other things to be taken away from the original writings. The Bible warns us not to do this in Revelation 22:18–19. Those of us who speak more than one language know how hard it is to translate something word for word into another language. It often sounds pretty funny. I don't think that Revelation is talking about language translation. If it was, most of us would never have been able to read God's Word for ourselves. I believe it means we shouldn't add or subtract from the meaning of the words and enforce added rules that aren't biblical.

For example, many scholars have deeply studied the information given about the return of Christ and the end times. Some have ventured to predict a certain date based on their research. Jesus said, *"No one knows about that day or hour, not even the angels in heaven, nor the Son, but only the Father"* (Matthew 24:36). Predicting a date for the return of Christ could be considered adding to what is written in God's Word. Some teach that there is no hell, when the Bible clearly talks about it (Matthew 5:22, Luke 16:23, and Revelation 20:14). This could be considered taking away from what is written in God's Word.

Really, we don't know who did the best job in accurate translation. All we can do is trust the Holy Spirit to help us understand. If people made mistakes, it is something God will deal with; it really isn't our concern. I am just very thankful that I don't have to learn a new language in order to read the Bible. I am grateful that others have taken the time to interpret God's Word into my language so that I can read and understand it for myself, without constantly checking the dictionary.

The most important thing to remember is that we need to know the author of God's Word. We can study all we want, memorize the Scripture in ten languages, and know everything there is to know about the Bible, and still not know Jesus Christ as Lord and Saviour. While Jesus was under persecution by religious leaders, He told them, *"You diligently study the Scriptures because you think that by them you possess eternal life. These are the Scriptures that testify about me, yet you refuse to come to me to have life"* (John 5:39–40). The Bible might be hard to understand at times, but its basic message, the good news about Jesus coming to save the world, is easy enough for a child to understand. In fact, Jesus told us to change and become more like children in order to enter the kingdom of Heaven (Matthew 18:3). Our childlike faith and trust in Jesus and His finished work on the cross are all we need to be part of God's family. Jesus is the only way to eternal life, and Scripture shows us the way (John 14:6).

Our one and only enemy, Satan, is the master of confusion. If he can keep Christians busy debating which Bible translation is the most accurate, he quite successfully keeps them from actually reading God's Word and applying it to their hearts and lives. I'm sure he also gloats every time a new believer buys an easy-reading Bible and quits reading it because someone tells them that they are reading an inferior version. Usually these opinions are passed from one person to another without evidence or fact.

No matter which translation we choose to read, the message to apply to our life is similar. John 13:34–35 tells us that we will be recognized as Jesus' disciples because of the love we show to others. Matthew 7:12 and Luke 6:31 tell us that the Law and the Prophets are summed up in doing unto others as we want them to do to us. Matthew 25:34–46 points out that whatever we did or did not do for one of the least of these, we did or did not do for Jesus.

Whatever we do, we should not throw away our faith because someone tells us that we are reading the wrong Bible. Jesus loves us. He died on the cross so that everyone in the whole world might have eternal life if they choose to believe in Him. We can read our Bibles and allow His love and the Holy Spirit to fill our hearts. We can trust that what we are reading is true; it does not have the opposite meaning in Greek. Remember that it is the author of the Bible that matters, not the language in which it is written, as He has made them all. We can enjoy our Bibles, but we shouldn't be afraid to purchase an easy-reading version if we find we have a hard time understanding the ones that have been gathering dust on our shelves for years. The Lord will use any or all of these Bibles to teach us what we need to know and draw us ever closer.

CHAPTER FIVE

DRESSING "RIGHT" FOR CHRIST

"CAN YOU BELIEVE THE CLOTHES PEOPLE WEAR nowadays?" The woman sitting beside me was pointing to a young girl facing us on the Edmonton city bus. "Makes you wonder what this world is coming to," she continued in a loud, self-righteous whisper.

I was at a loss for words and lamely mumbled something that could have been mistaken for agreement. It was my first time ever riding the city bus, and I had been thankful for the friendly lady who started a conversation at the bus stop. She had handed me a tract about God's salvation plan. I admired her courage and told her I was also a Christian. Now, a few minutes into the bus ride, my heart saddened as it dawned on me that the clothing issue among Christians wasn't confined to my hometown. It's an issue that has confused people since before Jesus walked the earth.

What exactly does clothing have to do with Christianity? Why have many churches enforced a certain dress code within their congregations? The explanation given to me as a young girl was that we had to dress differently from the world around us in order to be recognized as Christians. Jesus said that His disciples would be recognized by the love they show to others (John 13:34–35). He said we were to be the salt of the earth and the light of the world (Matthew 5:13–16).

Salt is essential for the flavour in our food but never visible to the naked eye when an ingredient in a recipe. We are quick to complain when the cook forgets to salt the soup. We also don't appreciate too much salt all at once. I once added a cup of salt to a jug of Kool-Aid instead of sugar, by mistake, and it tasted awful! We couldn't drink it, had to throw the whole thing out. Our lives need to make a positive difference in the lives of others, not be a rude dose of salt overload, so that they throw out the whole idea of Christianity because of our words and actions.

Light illuminates everything around it, but never stands out like a sore thumb. When we get lost in the dark woods and see a light in the distance, we know in which direction to go. Jesus wanted our love for others to be the salt and light that would draw them to God. He wants us to love instead of hate, encourage rather than complain. We are always to be a contrast to the attitude of darkness around us. He wants us to be like sunshine in the lives of others, being a blessing to those we know.

Clothing was already an issue when Jesus was teaching His disciples and the crowds that followed Him around. Jesus encouraged the people not to worry about what they would eat or how they should dress. He said, *"Why do you worry about clothes? See how the lilies of the field grow. They do not labor or spin. Yet I tell you that not even Solomon in all his splendor was dressed like one of these. If that is how God clothes the grass of the field, which is here today and tomorrow is thrown into the fire, will he not much more clothe you, O you of little faith?"* (Matthew 6:28–30) He said, *"Pagans run after all these things, and your heavenly Father knows that you need them. But seek first his kingdom and his righteousness, and all these things will be given to you as well"* (Matthew 6:32–33).

As believers, we are not exempt from the need of clothing. Jesus encourages us to trust God to provide for our needs and not run after those things as the pagans do, making a big deal about what we wear. Most of the dilemma we see about clothing today has nothing to do with being naked and in need of covering for warmth. The controversy is about which style is modest enough, whether or not a woman should be allowed to wear pants, etc. Jesus encouraged the people to trust God to provide and not be overly concerned about clothing, the way unbelievers are.

Believers in Paul's day were encouraged to dress modestly with decency and propriety, not with braided hair, jewellery, or expensive clothes, but with good deeds (1 Timothy 2:9–10). According to the dictionary, to be modest is to have the tendency to avoid praise or credit, being humble, unpretentious, not grand or showy, simple, having a regard for propriety. Propriety is the quality of being proper or appropriate, conformity with what is proper with socially accepted standards of manners and conduct. In other words, propriety simply means to fit in with those around us, and dressing appropriately for the occasion. For example, if it is thirty degrees below zero outside, you probably need to wear warm clothing. Common sense tells us that bare legs aren't appropriate in cold climates for long periods of time. Neither are fur coats appropriate in thirty-degree Celsius weather.

Peter encourages women to have the inward beauty of a gentle and quiet spirit, and not to be concerned over outward appearance. He wants women to win their husbands with their personality rather than their attire (1 Peter 3:1–4).

47

The church in which I grew up had a dress code, and it was especially strict when it came to women and girls. Hair had to be braided, jewellery was forbidden, and clothes had to be plain and sewn by the woman of the home. My mom used to spend hours at her sewing machine, making dresses for herself and four growing girls. Money was often scarce, so she would take apart clothes that didn't fit anymore and turn them into new dresses.

Modesty includes being able to appreciate clothes from the thrift store, and accepting hand-me-downs. Moms shouldn't have to worry about sewing everything for their families, especially while the children are small and need so much help in all other areas already. Children are only little once, and we have just one opportunity to train and teach them in the ways of God. While it is important to teach our children to be modest and cover themselves, the minute we define modesty as being a certain style, we lose the meaning of the word—just like Jesus, Paul, and Peter meant to take people's focus off of their clothing. However, many people have done the exact opposite with the same passage of Scripture and made clothing a vital part of their faith.

But then there is common sense again. We've all heard stories about a rapist who goes free because a woman was partly at fault due to her dress, or lack thereof. As Christian men and women, we need to be concerned about the effect we have on others. Do we dress with a desire to create lust? Are we taking precautions for our own safety's sake? Again, this is where propriety comes in, dressing appropriately for the occasion. For example, a swimsuit is fine for the beach or swimming pool, but not suitable for most other occasions.

Another concern in many cultures is the difference in men's and ladies' clothing. In my hometown, pants were considered men's clothing and not acceptable attire for women. The Old Testament does say that men shouldn't wear women's clothing, and women shouldn't wear men's clothing, and that we shouldn't wear clothing woven from more than one kind of material (Deuteronomy 22:5–11, and Leviticus 19:19). However, these passages do not define gender clothing, and proper attire for men and women varies in different countries. In Japan, kimonos are common for all, while in Nigeria everyone wears loose-fitting robes. Arab tribesmen in northern Africa use long flowing robes for protection from the intense heat of the sun. The cloaks mentioned in Deuteronomy 22:12 sound quite fancy with tassels on all four corners, but it doesn't specify if they were for the men or for the women. Dorcas sewed robes and other clothing for the poor (Acts 9:39), giving the indication that robes were still common in New Testament times.

Therefore, having established the fact that our apparel is not a big deal to God, should we as Christians impose our standard of dress on others? Should the issue of how to dress cause peer pressure among Christians, just as the issue of dress causes peer pressure among teens and pagans?

The truth is, not everyone has the same standards and definitions as to the meaning of the words "modesty," "decency," and "propriety." Although most people know that these words basically mean to cover ourselves with clothing that is acceptable to our general community, some people don't. Even when we try on an outfit in the store, we don't always know how it will look once we actually wear it. We stand in front of the mirror and have a very limited view of how we look in different poses. What do others see when I bend over to pick up something from the floor? What does the preacher see during his Sunday morning message when he stands up on stage behind the pulpit and has a bird's eye view looking down at the people? I imagine it must be hard to concentrate on God's Word when he sees a lot of cleavage staring back at him. It's no wonder many church leaders have defined modesty for their congregations by enforcing certain clothing styles. They do have the people's well-being in mind.

The Bible, however, gives us a lot of freedom as to how to dress. Even though some congregations choose to adopt a certain style of clothing for their members, it is their choice, not a direct instruction from God's Word. They have the right to choose what to wear, just like everyone else.

The Bible does give us specific directions as to how to clothe our hearts, giving instruction to clothe ourselves with compassion, kindness, humility, gentleness, and patience. It says to *"put on love, which binds them all together in perfect unity"* (Colossians 3:14). This is apparel for the heart, which is what really matters to Christ. When we are in Christ, seeking first His kingdom and His righteousness, the rest of our lives will fall into place quite naturally, including guidance as to which clothing is appropriate for which occasion.

God's will for us is to love as He loves, being His disciples in a love-starved world. The lady on the bus and myself had no right to gossip about someone else's choice of clothing, especially when we had no idea if the girl was even a Christian living according to biblical standards. What if she was interested in Christ previously, but due to overhearing our thoughtless words she lost all desire to learn more about Him?

As Christians, we should be able to look others in the eye and say hello without ever noticing how they are dressed. Let us truly be "the salt of the earth," our hearts dressed with the love of Christ, recognizable only by this love, modestly blending in with those around us all the while making the positive difference that salt should always make.

CHAPTER SIX

JUST ONE DRINK

"BUT WHERE DOES IT SAY THAT I CAN'T HAVE ONE social drink?" Burt threw up his hands in frustration. He had been attending a class in order to learn more about the Bible and how to live a Christian life. Everyone had always told him that drinking alcoholic beverages was not a Christian thing to do, yet the church celebrated communion using bread and wine. He was confused, and the teacher just kept on giving him passages about drunkenness, and how bad it was.

"Burt, maybe you just aren't ready to commit to living for Christ yet," answered the teacher, equally frustrated. "Why don't you pray about it, and I'm sure that in time the Lord will answer your question."

Have you ever been in Burt's shoes? Have you ever studied the Bible looking for the answer to this question, or asked an older Christian? If you have studied the Bible, you might know that Jesus made wine at a wedding (John 2:1–10), that Paul told Timothy to stop drinking only water and use a little wine because of his stomach problems (1 Timothy 5:23), and yes, Burt was right, many churches do use wine to celebrate communion in following our Lord's example, remembering His death (Luke 22:17–20 and 1 Corinthians 11:23–26).

However, the Bible also warns against drunkenness, and says, *"Wine is a mocker and beer a brawler; whoever is led astray by them is not wise"* (Proverbs 20:1). It also says, *"Who has woe? Who has sorrow? Who has strife? Who has complaints? Who has needless bruises? Who has bloodshot eyes? Those who linger over wine, who go to sample bowls of mixed wine. Do not gaze at wine when it is red, when it sparkles in the cup, when it goes down smoothly! In the end it bites like a snake and poisons like a viper"* (Proverbs 23:29–32; see also Proverbs 23:20–21, Luke 21:34, Romans 13:13, 1 Corinthians 6:9–10, Ephesians 5:18, 1 Thessalonians 5:6–11, and 1 Peter 4:1–4).

You probably already knew that being in a state of drunkenness is definitely not recommended. But what about that one social drink? Since Jesus made wine at a wedding, it should be permissible to have a social drink now and then, shouldn't it?

Paul told us about the freedom we have as believers. He said, *"'Everything is permissible'—but not everything is beneficial. 'Everything is permissible'—but not everything is constructive. Nobody should seek his own good, but the good of others… So whether you eat or drink or whatever you do, do it all for the glory of God. Do not cause anyone to stumble, whether Jews, Greeks, or the church of God"* (1 Corinthians 10:23–24,31–32).

I think this means that God trusts us to use the brains He gave us to judge for ourselves whether that one drink will harm us or help us. Is it beneficial or destructive? How does it affect others? We can use common sense to discern how our one drink affects those around us. A recovering alcoholic might slide right back to square one of his rehabilitation if he has just one drink. If I care about his health and well-being, I might think twice about tempting him in this way, and have my one drink later when he is not around.

One drink can mean the difference between life and death. I remember as if it were yesterday the anguished numbness I felt when I received the news on the telephone. My sixteen-year-old cousin had died in a car accident. There had to be some mistake! It just couldn't be true! We rushed to the hospital, only to find out that it was indeed true. She had just received her driver's license, and her parents had consented to her driving their pickup truck that fateful Sunday afternoon. She had picked up a few friends, socialized with a few more, and had alcohol to drink. Whether she had one drink or a few, we don't know. It was enough to impair her judgment and cause an accident that claimed her life.

We probably all know someone who died as a result of drunk driving. We probably all know a family or two where the marriage suffers due to alcohol abuse. We have heard of children being neglected and going hungry due to a parent's alcoholism. We might even know someone who is crippled for life due to an accident with a drunk driver.

Health statistics show how prolonged alcohol abuse affects the body, slowly destroying the liver, causing heart problems, brain damage, impotence, etc. The Bible tells us that our body is a temple of the Holy Spirit and that we are supposed to honour God with it (1 Corinthians 6:19–20). When we deliberately abuse our bodies, we are definitely not honouring God.

Back to our question, where does it say in the Bible that I can't have one social drink? The answer is, nowhere. This is why Christian leaders struggle so much with giving people like Burt a complete answer. Most of them know only too well where that "one drink" leads, and to say that you are allowed to have it puts the person at risk to possible long-term problems with alcoholism.

I want to share one more portion of Scripture which has often helped me come to terms with these gray areas of life which do not have simple yes or no answers.

> The acts of the sinful nature are obvious: sexual immorality, impurity and debauchery, idolatry and witchcraft; hatred, discord, jealousy, fits of rage, selfish ambition, dissentions, factions and envy; drunkenness, orgies, and the like. I warn you, as I did before, that those who live like this will not inherit the kingdom of God. But the fruit of the Spirit is love, joy, peace, patience, kindness, goodness, faithfulness, gentleness and self-control. Against such things there is no law. (Galatians 5:19–23)

So what fruits grow in your life after you have had that one drink? Does it sometimes lead to just one more, and then another? If this is the case, you probably don't remember a lot of what the aftereffects of your one drink are. In this case, you might have to ask the people who witnessed your actions and hope they will be honest and tell you the truth. Maybe you don't even want to know the truth about it, as it might be embarrassing. In extreme cases, your actions might have led you to becoming a co-parent with someone you don't even know; your child is the one who ends up living with the consequences of your actions.

Did the fruit of your actions bring forth love, joy, peace, patience, kindness, goodness, faithfulness, gentleness, and self-control? Or did your actions bring forth sexual immorality, hatred, jealousy, fits of rage, and drunkenness?

Only I and the people closest to me know the results of my social drink. As a Christian with Jesus in my heart, I only want what is best for the ones I love and care about. Jesus loves us and only wants what is best for us. He really prefers not to watch us suffer from liver disease a few years down the road, which is why the Bible encourages us not to indulge in too much wine. Many churches have even switched from wine to grape juice for communion services, because they do not want to tempt the recovering alcoholic to have that one more drink.

While Jesus was on earth, He was accused of being a glutton and a drunkard, a friend to tax collectors and sinners (Matthew 11:19 and Luke 7:34). He cared more about these people than about His own reputation. He was indeed a friend to sinners, and He still is today. He continually calls people from their sinful ways and turns them into saints, as the result of them simply putting their faith in Him and His finished work on the cross.

Just like parents try to encourage their children to live good lives, Jesus wants us to live for our own well-being. As a Mom, I will always love my children, no matter what they do. It gives me great joy to see them happy and doing well. If, however, they should end up in prison as a result of breaking the law, or addicted to alcohol and suffering the consequences, I know my heart would weep for them, wanting so much for them to stop hurting and live happily again. The Bible says that if we, being evil, know how to give good gifts to our children, how much more will our heavenly Father give good gifts to those who ask Him? (Matthew 7:11)

Our Lord loves us more than we as parents are capable of loving our own children. He desires to see us happy and doing well. It grieves Him when we insist on deliberately destroying the body He gave us. Alcohol also hurts our families who love us and is often a stumbling block in our witness to others when we proclaim to be Christians.

It doesn't take a genius to figure out that most of the time, alcohol produces more negative results than positive ones. Although one drink may start out innocently enough, beware lest you fall into the trap that has caught so many others. Alcohol can start as a casual social thing to do, but alas, a few years down the road, you may realize too late that you're addicted and can't stop. Weigh the options. Yes, you are allowed to have a drink. It is not forbidden. But is it beneficial or destructive in your life? You be the judge.

CHAPTER SEVEN

GROW UP AND LET GO

"DAD, I HAVE A REAL PROBLEM WITH YOU DATING that widow at your age! I heard she never gave her children any inheritance, even though her husband left her plenty. I think she's just after your money!"

These are strong words, but they are statements often made by adult children whose widowed parents dare to start a relationship with a potential step-parent.

Where I come from, churches even have rules that apply to widows and widowers when they get remarried. The general rule of thumb is that before the widowed can get remarried, they first have to sell everything they own and give half of the proceeds to their children, even if the children are self-supporting adults. This causes many lonely seniors to remain single, even when they receive a marriage proposal.

Although this rule is not written down or preached, widowed people often find out the hard way after their spouse passes on. If someone leaves behind a will that does not follow expected tradition, their spouse is rejected by the community, simply for accepting the provision left them by their deceased spouse.

What exactly does the Bible teach about this? On what principle are these traditions founded?

First of all, the Bible defines a marriage as a man leaving his parent's household and uniting with his wife to become one flesh. The husband and wife are no longer two, but one, starting their own family unit (see Genesis 2:24, Matthew 19:4–6, and Ephesians 5:31). This means that the parents are no longer responsible to meet the needs of their adult children, and the young couple is no longer responsible for childhood chores in their parents' home. They are now Mr. and Mrs. Independent, instead of sons and daughters of Mr. and Mrs. Parent. This doesn't mean they have to stop helping or caring for one another as extended family, it just means that the responsibilities have changed. A new marriage commitment has been made, a new household has been created.

The next time these responsibilities change is if and when the parents become elderly and need help taking care of themselves, especially if one passes on and the other parent is widowed. Paul encouraged Timothy to give proper recognition to those widows who were really in need, but if the widow had children and grandchildren, the family should put their religion into practice by caring for their own family, thus repaying their parents and grandparents (1 Timothy 5:3–4).

Secondly, the Bible teaches that a husband is responsible for taking care of the needs of his wife, as he is instructed to love her as Christ loved the church. The wife is instructed to be submissive to her husband and to be his helper in what he does (see Genesis 2:18 and Ephesians 5:22–29).

This marriage covenant is valid until one partner is taken away in death. It ends when one partner dies, as there is no marriage in heaven. The surviving partner is then free to marry another believer, if he or she so desires (see Matthew 22:23–33 and 1 Corinthians 7:39). In fact, younger widows are encouraged to marry again (1 Timothy 5:11–16).

So what does the Bible teach about issues of inheritance? The truth is, there is little direct teaching on the subject. We can, however, look at the facts on marriage and conclude that husbands and wives do become one, and therefore their combined property becomes their joint estate. When two people marry, their expenses generally go down, as they now only need one house instead of two, one vehicle, one utility bill, etc. In the case of the lonely widower, he now enjoys home-cooked meals again and doesn't need to go to restaurants as often. The family's burden for the widowed parent decreases, as they know their loved one is no longer alone and desolate, but has a companion and helpmate.

In the Old Testament, we have a few examples of fathers leaving something for their sons when they die. Abraham left everything he owned to his son Isaac, but while he was still alive he gave gifts to the sons of his concubines. Sarah had passed on before Abraham, and the Bible doesn't tell us if his second wife Keturah was still alive when he died (Genesis 23, 25:1–11). Ishmael was Abraham's firstborn son, born to him by Sarah's maidservant Hagar (Genesis 16).

After Isaac grew old and was close to the end of his life, he only had one birthright and blessing to give to one of his twin boys. Since Esau was born first, he was to receive it. However, Esau sold his birthright to Jacob in exchange for supper one day, and Jacob tricked his father Isaac into blessing him instead of Esau (Genesis 25:21–34 and Genesis 27).

In the New Testament, we have a situation where a man wasn't happy with how his father's inheritance was divided.

> Someone in the crowd said to him, "Teacher, tell my brother to divide the inheritance with me."
> Jesus replied, "Man, who appointed me a judge or an arbiter between you?" Then he said to them, "Watch out! Be on your guard against all kinds of greed; a man's life does not consist in the abundance of his possessions." (Luke 12:13–15)

Jesus went on to tell them the parable of the rich fool who tore down his storage barns and built bigger ones so that he could store his abundant crop for a few years and take life easy for awhile. *"But God said to him, 'You fool! This very night your life will be demanded from you. Then who will get what you have prepared for yourself?' This is how it will be for anyone who stores up things for himself but is not rich toward God"* (Luke 12:20–21). He then encouraged them not to worry about their lives but to seek God's kingdom, and all these things would be given to them as well (Luke 12:22–34 and Matthew 6:19–34).

Our research confirms that although Scripture gives us examples of how various people throughout history dealt with their possessions when they died, there were never rules as to how it should be done. It seems that this is one choice that has always been made by the individual. It doesn't seem quite fair when we look in at a distance. We would think that Isaac could have given both of his sons a blessing, especially after he received everything his father Abraham owned when he died, even though Ishmael was the older brother. Abraham probably gave everything to Isaac because he knew that it wasn't wise to leave more than one owner in control of a property. He had, however, given to his other children while he was still alive. Perhaps Isaac also received the responsibility of maintaining the family along with the inheritance. Proverbs says, *"A good man leaves an inheritance for his children's children"* (Proverbs 13:22) and *"A wise servant will rule over a disgraceful son, and will share the inheritance as one of the brothers"* (Proverbs 17:2).

The thing to remember is that inheritance and blessings are given as gifts; they are not something we should expect or demand. We should never count our chickens before they hatch, or take ownership of other people's possessions, even if they have promised them to us. It only becomes ours after it is actually given to us.

James tells us, *"Religion that God our Father accepts as pure and faultless is this: to look after orphans and widows in their distress and to keep oneself from being polluted by the world"* (James 1:27). Jesus said, *"Beware of the teachers of the law. They like to walk around in flowing robes and love to be greeted in the marketplaces and have the most important seats in the synagogues and the places of honor at banquets. They devour widows' houses and for a show make lengthy prayers. Such men will be punished most severely"* (Luke 20:46–47; see also Matthew 23:14 and Mark 12:40).

How could someone devour a widow's house? Might they possibly have taken ownership of it and sold the home and everything in it, then divided up the money among whoever they felt should have it? However they did it, Jesus did not approve of this practice.

Our responsibility is to make sure that the needs of widows and orphans are met, using our own finances or the church's (Acts 6:1–6 and James 1:27). It has never been the responsibility of church leaders to make up rules as to how estates should be divided, or to change people's last wills after they are gone in order to follow manmade traditions. Jesus gave us a perfect example to follow when He stayed out of the situation in Luke 12:13–15.

When a married person dies, the surviving spouse is left behind to carry the load that two used to carry together. He or she now carries the full responsibility of earning a living and taking care of the family and the household duties formerly shared by both. Many couples cannot imagine the pain of losing each other and invest in a life insurance policy in the hopes of easing their partner's pain and workload when this happens. I always feel that I would want my husband and family to at least have time off of work so that they could heal and take counselling if need be. What if they were so devastated that they were unable to work and they ended up losing their home for lack of payment?

According to the traditions of our ancestors, if my husband were to die, I would have to sell everything we own, pay all debt, and put half of the proceeds into a trust account for our children. I would then have to buy or rent a new home and raise the children on the other half. In the case of a young family, it would probably mean they would live on in poverty. The remaining parent would have to work twice as hard to make ends meet, leaving little time for parenting.

Mrs. Dell was obedient to the tradition of her church after her husband died, even though she never married again. She sold what they had and divided half of it among her children. Her youngest son was quite rebellious at the time, and into wild living. He spent his inheritance on drugs and alcohol and nearly killed himself in the process. To this day, he still has health problems and cannot work to support his wife and family. Mrs.

Dell loved her children and respected and followed her church's tradition, but her son's life was actually damaged as a result.

In closing, I want to say that children do need to grow up and leave home sometime. As adults, they need to be able to look after themselves. How Mom and Dad choose to live and spend their money is really none of their concern, unless of course the parents are no longer capable of making these decisions for themselves. We need to let go of our parents and allow them to pursue their own happiness, just as much as we need to allow our children to grow up and become responsible adults.

CHAPTER EIGHT

RECOGNIZING OUR ENEMY

"DO YOU HAVE ANY HAIR SPRAY, MARIE?" ROGER
was doing his hair and he wanted it to be "just so," as appearance meant everything.

"No, we don't," responded Marie. Inwardly, she was fuming.
How did he have the nerve to ask for hairspray when they hardly
had food to put on the table? How could this stranger expect to
have everything provided for him when he couldn't be bothered
to take the job he had been offered? He had already worn out his
welcome. He had asked to spend the night, and here he was, six
weeks later, still taking advantage of their hospitality.

Marie and Frank had always believed in an "open door"
policy, being hospitable and welcoming to whoever happened
to knock on their door. They believed in applying the verse that
said, *"Do not forget to entertain strangers, for by so doing some people
have entertained angels without knowing it"* (Hebrews 13:2). They
wanted to share what God provided, but this was a little bit
much.

"Marie, you know what the Bible says about God loving a
cheerful giver," taunted a voice in Marie's thoughts. "You are

sharing what you have, but you aren't being cheerful about it, so God must hate you!"

Marie knew the thought came from Satan, and she fought to overcome it. Although she got victory, he repeatedly attacked her with similar thoughts, trying to get her down again and again. This went on for several weeks.

One morning, Marie woke up with a Bible verse running through her head— *"My grace is sufficient for you"* (2 Corinthians 12:9). It took a few minutes for the message to register, but when it did, Marie was filled with joy. Yes! We are saved by grace, not by works! Our works have nothing to do with our salvation, or how much God loves us. We are saved by the blood of Jesus alone, and nothing can separate us from His love! (John 3:16–18, Romans 8:28–39, and Ephesians 2:8–9) God's grace really is sufficient! Marie was excited, and she overcame her inner struggle with the enemy. The blood of Jesus gave the victory, as the Lord planted in her mind the verse she needed to overcome Satan's attack.

The Bible tells us that Satan is, indeed, the accuser of believers, and accuses us before God. He leads the whole world astray and makes war against those who believe and obey God's commandments (Revelation 12:9–17). He prowls around looking for someone to devour, and often masquerades as an angel of light (2 Corinthians 11:14 and 1 Peter 5:8). We are, indeed, soldiers in a spiritual battle when we follow Christ. The Bible says that *"everyone who wants to live a godly life in Christ Jesus will be persecuted"* (2 Timothy 3:12) and *"Our struggle is not against flesh and blood, but against the rulers, against the authorities, against the powers of this dark world and against the spiritual forces of evil in the heavenly realms"* (Ephesians 6:12). Other people (flesh and blood) are not our enemies, although Satan will try to make it appear as if they are in order to keep them from receiving love from Christ's followers.

Fortunately, God has also given us spiritual armour with which to overcome the devil's schemes. We have the belt of truth, which affirms our faith and helps us recognize lies. This helps us whenever Satan pretends to be an angel of light and tries to discourage us with partial truths. In Marie's case, he used a partial truth to attack her. The truth he whispered was, "God loves a cheerful giver." The lie was, "He hates you." We have the breastplate of righteousness, which I believe is the blood of Jesus. His blood is our only righteousness, the only sacrifice sufficient to take away our sins and make us clean. Our feet are fitted with the readiness that comes from the gospel of peace—we are soldiers of love and peace, living peaceably with others as much as possible. We have the shield of faith, with which we can extinguish all the flaming arrows of the evil one. This shield helps us not to take things personally, but to expect attacks from Satan and be prepared for them, even when they come from the people we are trying to reach with the love of Christ. We have the helmet of salvation, which protects our thoughts and reassures us that we are saved by God's grace. This helmet is what the Holy Spirit used to remind Marie that she was saved by grace, not by her works. Last but not least, we have the sword of the Spirit, which is the Word of God. When we know God's Word, we are able to recognize half-truths and lies and live a victorious life (Ephesians 6:11–17).

Satan sometimes uses little parts of the Bible and twists them in order to confuse us. He even tried this on Jesus, after He had been fasting in the desert for forty days. He took Jesus to the holy city and had Him stand on the highest point of the temple.

"If you are the Son of God," he said, "throw yourself down. For it is written: 'He will command his angels concerning you, and they will lift you up in their hands, so that you will not strike your foot against a stone.'"

Jesus answered him, "It is also written: 'Do not put the Lord your God to the test.'" (Matthew 4:6–7)

You see, Jesus knew God's Word and recognized the twist. Yes, God does send angels to protect us from danger, but it is not to be used when we don't need it. It is not something we should test God with, or use like a magic act.

When I think of war, I envision the game of Prisoner's Base—except on a larger scale. Prisoner's Base consists of two teams. Both teams have to capture as many of the other team's players as possible, and take them "hostage" in their own turf. The remaining team members have to be brave and tag their team (one at a time) behind enemy lines in order to rescue them from the enemy's grasp, without getting caught themselves. Whoever captures all of the rival team's players first wins the game. The interesting thing with this game is that as long as both teams stay safely within their own zone, there is really no fight or challenge. The minute one team captures someone from the other team, however, the fight is on to rescue that player.

One of Satan's tactics is to keep believers busy at home, and at church, debating over issues and never being instrumental in freeing the prisoners he has taken captive. Don't get me wrong: it is important for us to fellowship with other believers and work within the church. It's just that sometimes we get caught up with non-essentials, forgetting our purpose for being here and those who desperately need to know that Jesus loves them.

As believers and soldiers of Christ, we are commissioned by our Lord to win unbelievers to Him, converting them to our side, simply by them repenting from their sins, accepting salvation, and becoming God's children. Our only weapon is love, freely given to us by Christ on the cross, in order for it to overflow to others through the Holy Spirit. When the Lord's servant shows love in this way, by being kind and peaceable and not quarrelling about every little thing, there is hope that his opponents will come to a knowledge of the truth and escape from the trap of the devil, who has taken them captive to do his will (2 Timothy 2:24–26).

Satan doesn't want to lose his captives and will do his utmost to prevent the believers from making contact with them, lest those unbeliever come to believe in Jesus. He knows that a believer is secure in Christ, and he can't really capture him or her, so he tries his best to keep believers from rescuing others and bringing them to the Lord.

If we, as soldiers of Christ, reach forth a hand of love to an unbeliever, we can expect a flaming arrow to come our way. In these times, we need to put our shield of faith in place so that we won't be hurt. These flaming arrows are sometimes emotional ones, and might come in various forms.

I have often found that I was down and depressed after sharing the Lord's Word with someone the day before. Sometimes others will give us a cold shoulder or say hurtful things about us after we have shared God's Word with them, because they are under conviction due to the Holy Spirit drawing them (John 16:8). Sometimes they will ignore or hurt us in order to make the conviction stop. In these times, we truly need to remember who the enemy is, and continue to gently and patiently love these people in our personal mission fields.

It is comforting to remember that God is always stronger than Satan, and is always in control. Even when Jesus was tempted by the devil in the desert, it was the Spirit who had led Him there, specifically for that purpose (Matthew 4:1). In Job, we read about how God allowed Satan to test Job, but only to a point (see Job 1–2, especially Job 1:12 and Job 2:6). We can rest assured knowing that nothing will happen to us that isn't within God's control.

Jesus is Lord, and no one can say that except by the Holy Spirit (1 Corinthians 12:3). I once had a spiritual attack in my sleep, or in my dream. I remember thinking, *Say "Jesus is Lord," and you will gain victory.* I woke up as if half-drowning, gasping, struggling to say it, and I did once I awoke. Satan has to flee when we praise Jesus, and it gives us victory.

Therefore, onward Christian soldiers! We are indeed at war! Jesus already won the victory, so we have nothing to fear! As brave soldiers daring to cross enemy lines in order to rescue the perishing, we will be attacked. Rejoice! For with every attack from the enemy, we know that we have made progress in reaching someone for Christ.

CHAPTER NINE

WE ARE IN THE WORLD, BUT NOT OF THE WORLD

MARIEREADTHENOTEWITHDISBELIEF.SHECOULDN'T believe it. Her gentle little boy had received detention at school because he had thrown sand at another little boy, and they had both been disciplined. It was true; Jeremy had been encouraged by his dad to defend himself if others kept picking on him. Marie herself had told him he was allowed to stand up for himself, but that he should never start a fight.

What was a parent to do? Jeremy had been coming home upset quite regularly in the past month because of how Billy had treated him. Frank and had Marie tried their best to teach their children to love others in following Christ's example, but at the same time they also knew that sometimes a bully has to be shown that the people he picks on can stand up for themselves. As it turned out, the two boys spent a week of noon hours together in the detention room, and became friends. Not best friends, of course, but friends enough to invite one another to their birthday parties and socialize occasionally. More importantly, the teasing and bullying stopped and the situation was properly reconciled.

These types of situations are what cause people to separate themselves from the world around them. Today, more and more people are home-schooling their children in order to protect them from these types of complications, teaching them only what the parents see fit.

For many years, people have literally left well-populated areas and moved their families into the middle of nowhere, because they feared their children would fall into sin if they were tempted by too many worldly things around them. Do you suppose this is what the Bible means when it tells us to be separate or different from the world around us? (2 Corinthians 6:14–18)

Many people think so. Many have moved halfway across the world from Canada to Mexico to Bolivia, and back again, trying to find a place where they could live separately from the world. The trouble was, their sinful nature moved with them, and wherever they went a part of the world came right along with them. They found they could not flee from all the sinful temptations around them, as each place presented new temptations to deal with. They had to learn to live in the world without succumbing to it.

The Bible tells us that *"the cravings of sinful man, the lust of his eyes and the boasting of what he has and does… comes not from the Father but from the world. The world and its desires pass away, but the man who does the will of God lives forever"* (1 John 2:16–17). Jesus told us that we are the salt and light of the world (Matthew 5:14–16). He said that we would have peace in Him, but that we would have trouble in this world. He told us to be encouraged because He had overcome the world (John 16:33). He actually sent His disciples out into the world, telling them to *"preach the good news to all creation"* (Mark 16:15).

How does this work? How can we be the light of the world, preach the good news to the world, and keep ourselves separate from the world, all at the same time? How can we be *in* the world, but not *of* the world?

Jesus told His disciples that people would recognize us as Christians by the love we show to others. He said we should love one another, as He loved us (John 13:34–35). How did He love us? *"God demonstrates his own love for us in this: While we were still sinners, Christ died for us"* (Romans 5:8). Since Jesus gave His life for us while we were sinners, we need to love others in this same sacrificial way. This means showing God's love to people while they are still sinners, in order to draw them to Christ. This means we need to associate with people who aren't Christians yet.

A good example of someone applying this is found in the story of the Good Samaritan. A priest and a Levite both passed by a hurt man lying naked on the road after being stripped, robbed, and beaten by thieves. Perhaps they were in a hurry, almost late for work or a meeting at church. Whatever the case, they walked on by without making any attempt to help the man. A Samaritan came by, helped the man onto his own donkey, and transported him to the nearest inn to take care of him. The next day, he gave the innkeeper extra money to take care of the man until he was well and told him he would reimburse him next time for any extra expenses he might incur (Luke 10:25–37). This Samaritan certainly showed mercy and love to his fellow man, being different from the world around him.

You see, the world won't help us unless we have money to pay, plus interest. When we don't have money to pay the electricity bill, the electric company turns off our power supply and the meat goes bad in the freezer. If we can no longer make the mortgage payments on our house, the bank repossesses it and we no longer have a home. The world as we know it is very cut and dry. There are no exceptions. When we as Christians are separate from the world, we will be different from the usual mode of doing things. We will show love and compassion instead of joining the rest of the world in stepping on someone who is already down.

Today, if we come upon a hurt man lying by the side of the road, it might only require a simple phone call to the police or ambulance in order to help. If we're close to home, we might accommodate him in our own house. Whatever the situation, we can follow the Samaritan's example of showing love and compassion. You see, the Good Samaritan wasn't out searching for someone to help that day. He simply responded to the situation that interrupted him on his way. Jesus encourages us to do the same as we travel our road, interacting with others on our journey.

I remember a parent-teacher interview I had with our daughter's teacher when she was in Grade Two. The teacher shared that once a week, she allowed the class to have lunch anywhere in the classroom, with friends of the student's choice. Our daughter, Marcella, was quite shy and usually sat with the same friends every week. However, one day there was a boy sitting all by himself with nobody to eat with. Marcella had noticed this and had asked if she could sit with him. She proceeded to have lunch with him instead of with her usual friends. The teacher shared this with me, and my heart was touched. Sometimes being separate from the world and preaching the Gospel message might be a simple act of love with no words required. On this occasion, a child gave up her weekly privilege of eating with her friends, because she noticed that someone else didn't have a friend. Jesus' love shone through her actions.

As we live in this world, God uses various methods to guide us, teach us, and discipline us as He continually looks after our well-being. We were studying the Lord's Prayer a while ago in a Bible study class. The question was asked, "Does God lead us into temptation?" (Matthew 6:13) Since God does not tempt anyone with evil (James 1:13), why did Jesus teach His disciples to pray this way, asking God not to lead them into temptation?

I believe this shows how wise, loving, and caring our Father in Heaven truly is. A young mother at the same Bible study class shared how her little boy was intrigued by heat and fire. When she told him "hot," he did not relate to the pain of being burned, so she was constantly on guard, protecting him from burning himself. One day she had a slightly cooled cup of tea, and she lured him to touch it. It was warm enough for him to feel heat, but not hot enough for him to burn himself. She used this to explain to him that it was hot, and that it might hurt him. From then on, whenever she said "No, hot," he withdrew his hand and listened.

I believe this is exactly how God teaches us. He doesn't tempt us Himself, but He allows us to be tempted by Satan so that we will learn to stay away from danger zones. He disciplines us in this way, guiding us into a close walk as we learn to trust Him, as He always has our best interest at heart.

When the Bible instructs the church to expel an immoral brother, it says to *"hand this man over to Satan, so that the sinful nature may be destroyed and his spirit saved on the day of the Lord"* (1 Corinthians 5:5). Even when using church discipline, the purpose of the procedure is for the person to realize that Satan's way isn't good, so that he will turn back and follow God's way again. Parents won't always be able to remove the hot cup of tea before the child pours it all over himself; they have to somehow teach the child to know for himself what is good for him, and slowly start trusting him to make the right choices in life.

My husband, Abe, was first drawn to the love of Christ when he went for a sleepover at his friend Harvey's house. When bedtime came, Harvey's Mom tucked the boys in and kissed them both goodnight. This simple act of love and acceptance left a warm glow on Abe's heart for years to come. He grew a desire to have a home like Harvey's, even though he didn't know exactly what it was that made Harvey's home so special. Many years later, during the boys' Grade Nine camping trip, this same Harvey and George (another Christian friend) witnessed to Abe about Christ, and he became a believer. If these two Christian boys hadn't been in Abe's class at the local public school, he might never have learned about Jesus and become a Christian. Over the years, our children have brought home many friends from school. Sometimes they have spent the weekend at our house and God has blessed us with the opportunity to take them to church. Occasionally, we have had the opportunity to witness about Christ to them, and prayed with them. Always, this has presented the opportunity to get to know them and to show forth love and kindness. If we had moved into the wilderness by ourselves, we wouldn't have had these opportunities for God to use as a vessel to share His love. If we as Christians huddle in a little group and associate only with other Christians, the lost will never experience the wonder of God's love and receive salvation through our witness of Christ's atoning blood.

As a mom, I can certainly understand the need to protect our children from the world out there. In fact, if I had done what I felt like doing and allowed "what-if" fears to overwhelm me, I would have kept my children as close to me as possible. The truth of the matter is that they grow up, and we grow older, and none of us have a guarantee as to how long we have to live on planet earth. Our children will probably outlive us. How will they survive if we teach them to depend only on us? We need to let our children experience a few storms in life while they are still young, while we are here to help them and guide them through it. This will strengthen them for the future when they have to leave the protective shelter of our greenhouse and face temptations and trials alone. With God's help, they will survive and be His salt and light within the world, while being separate from it.

Our third son, Lawrence, had just such a "storm" in his life during school one day when he was quite young. He came home and told me his woes, and I immediately felt sorry for him. I encouraged him to stand up for himself if he needed to. With tears in his eyes, he responded, "But Mom, what about loving our enemies? Remember what the Bible says?" I stood humbled and corrected, and very proud of my little guy. "Yes, Lawrence, you're right. Do what you can to be kind to the person who is hurting you, and I will be praying for you." We prayed for his "enemy" together, and when I asked him how things went over the next few days, things had improved.

Jesus gave us a wonderful example of how we can be different from the world, and reach the world with His love at the same time. When Jesus arrived in Jericho one day, a wealthy tax collector named Zacchaeus climbed up into a tree so that he might catch a glimpse of Jesus as He was passing by. *"When Jesus reached the spot, he looked up and said to him, "Zaccheaus, come down immediately. I must stay at your house today"* (Luke 19:5). Zaccheaus was filled with joy, and welcomed Him gladly, but the people who saw this—the world—began to mutter about Jesus being the guest of a sinner. Zaccheaus responded by vowing to give half of his possessions to the poor, and paying back wherever he had cheated anyone (Luke 19:1–9).

You see, Jesus didn't condemn Zaccheaus, although He knew full well who Zaccheaus was. He didn't say, "You better repent and change your ways or you'll end up in hell." Instead, Jesus honoured Zaccheaus by being his guest when the whole world despised and rejected him. This love gave Zaccheaus the desire to do right, and changed his heart. Jesus said, *"Today salvation has come to this house, because this man, too, is a son of Abraham. For the Son of Man came to seek and to save what was lost"* (Luke 19:9–10).

This must also be our mission, as we must walk as Jesus did (1 John 2:6). This is a definite challenge, as it takes courage to reach out in love to those who are despised by everyone else. This is our mission field. The people who are doing wrong and living in sin are potential brothers and sisters in Christ. Unless we love them as Jesus loved Zaccheaus, they might never know Christ and be saved. We must seek the lost in love.

Jesus said,

> But I tell you who hear me: Love your enemies, do good to those who hate you, bless those who curse you, pray for those who mistreat you. If someone strikes you on one cheek, turn to him

the other also. If someone takes your cloak, do not stop him from taking your tunic. Give to everyone who asks you, and if anyone takes what belongs to you, do not demand it back. Do to others as you would have them do to you. If you love those who love you, what credit is that to you? Even "sinners" love those who love them. And if you do good to those who are good to you, what credit is that to you? Even "sinners" do that. And if you lend to those from whom you expect repayment, what credit is that to you? Even "sinners" lend to "sinners," expecting to be repaid in full. But love your enemies, do good to them, and lend to them without expecting to get anything back. Then your reward will be great, and you will be sons of the Most High, because he is kind to the ungrateful and wicked. Be merciful, just as your Father is merciful. (Luke 6:27–36)

As people, we struggle with this. I keep a record of who sent me Christmas cards last year so that I can remember them next year. We feel bad accepting a gift without giving one in return. We feel we have to give back to people who give to us. We are usually very good at loving those who love us, just like the rest of the world.

We are called to love one another, but we truly do have an even higher calling as believers. We are called to love those who don't love us, even to the extent of loving our enemies and lending them our things without expecting to get them back. When we do this, the world will look at us and call us foolish

(1 Corinthians 1:18–30). After all, who in their right mind keeps on loving and giving when others just take advantage of it and never give anything back? But it is with the love of Christ flowing through us that the lost are drawn and saved for eternity. It is with His strength and the Holy Spirit within us that we can go on being His vessels of mercy and compassion to a lost and dying world.

Many feel that this work is only for those who are trained in Bible schools, and elected to church leadership. The apostle Paul, earlier known as Saul, had very little training, and no election by men. The Lord called him away from his life of destroying believers into serving Christ instead. Paul was blinded during this process, then healed, filled with the Holy Spirit, and baptized by Ananias. He started preaching immediately, without consulting any man (Acts 9:1–22 and Galatians 1:1–24). Paul had been extremely zealous in following the Judaism traditions of his fathers. Legally and traditionally, he had done everything right, including having been circumcised on the eighth day. He had a faultless, legalistic righteousness. After his conversion, he considered all that rubbish in order to gain Christ. He no longer had a righteousness of his own that came from the Law, but had a righteousness that came from God that is by faith (Philippians 3:4–9). He then focused on preaching Christ crucified (1 Corinthians 2:1–5).

The Lord doesn't call everyone as dramatically as He called Paul, but He does call us as His followers to go into the world and preach the good news to all creation, making disciples of all nations and baptizing them (Mark 16:15 and Matthew 28:19–20).

Not everyone is called to use the exact same method to make this happen, since we have been given different spiritual gifts with which to serve within the body of Christ (1 Corinthians

12:4–31 and Ephesians 4:11–12). Some are called to be pastors and teachers, while others are called to help and encourage others. There are countless ways to evangelize the world, from bringing food to a grieving family to showing appreciation to someone for being kind. We can use the gifts God has given us to be His vessels of love to others.

Paul went to many places on his missionary trips. While in Athens, he was quite disturbed by the many idols the people there worshipped. Instead of condemning them, he commented on how religious they were, and pointed out one of their own altars which had the inscription, "to an unknown God." He then proceeded to tell them about the "unknown" God, and shared the Gospel of Jesus Christ. Some sneered, but others became believers through his message (Acts 17:16–34).

Some people are called to other countries to spread the Gospel, like Paul, while others are told to spread the Word in their own towns (Mark 5:18–20). Wherever we are located, our world includes our workplace, our schools, the local grocery store, and wherever else we see other people. The people we meet are either fellow Christians in need of encouragement or future believers who need us to show them the love of Christ by our words and actions. The love of Christ within us is what makes us separate from the world around us, not our geographical location.

As believers, we are in this world as citizens of heaven, shining like stars in the universe. Our mission is to love as Jesus loved, so that others will want to know Him, too.

CHAPTER TEN

THE SIMPLIFIED LAW—LIVING IN LOVE

"HOW THEN SHALL WE LIVE?" LIZ ASKED. SHE WAS obviously frustrated. Her parents had taught her the Ten Commandments, along with culture, dress codes, and a few religious traditions. These had been passed on for a few generations and were the only things they knew.

Liz had been learning about God's grace and mercy towards sinners, and it just didn't make any sense. Liz had obeyed the rules she had been taught for as long as she could remember. How was it possible that a sinner could become righteous just like that? Why bother trying so hard to be good when the bad guy just had to repent and believe, thus becoming just as righteous as someone who had a long track record of good works?

Liz is not alone in her struggle. For many years, people have been confused between the Old Testament Law and the grace we read about in the New Testament. Which Old Testament laws are relevant today, and to what extent do we need to follow them?

Many Old Testament laws are similar to the rules of our country today. For example, there were laws governing sexual and marriage relationships, such as, *"No one is to approach any close relative to have sexual relations"* (Leviticus 18:6; see also verses 7–23). Today, incest is punished according to our Criminal Code.

There were also laws and regulations about how to be cleansed from infections, childbirth, mildew, and discharge (Leviticus 12–15). Many similar rules are practiced within the medical profession today, and we are often reminded that hand-washing prevents the spread of germs!

There were laws governing social responsibility, mercy, justice, and injuries (Exodus 21–23:19). In the case of a death or serious injury, law enforcers had to take life for life, eye for eye, bruise for bruise, etc. (Exodus 21:23–25). If a man stole an ox or a sheep, he had to pay back five head of cattle for the ox, or four sheep for the sheep (Exodus 22:1). Theft, murder, and violence are still punished in most countries today. It gives us a sense of security, knowing that law enforcers are on the job, and that law breakers aren't able to do whatever they desire without consequences.

Many Old Testament rules were beneficial, enabling the people to live longer and healthier lives. Sexual immorality does lead to various diseases, as do infections and uncleanliness. Thieves and murderers have always had to face consequences for their bad actions. These laws were given for the protection and benefit of the people, just like the laws of our land today are meant to protect and benefit everyone. The difference is that many of them are no longer enforced by priests and religious leaders, but by the courts and policemen of the land. The Bible tells us that we do need to submit to the governing authorities of our country, as they have been established by God (Romans 13:1–7).

Many people think of the Law as being synonymous with the Ten Commandments. These were given to Moses to pass onto the people, and are also part of the Law (Deuteronomy 5:1–22). The Ten Commandments were also meant to protect and benefit the people, making life easier for them.

However, we are not saved or righteous because we follow the rules. We are not justified by observing the Law, but by faith in Jesus Christ. Jesus died so that we could become righteous. If righteousness could have been gained through being obedient to the Law, Jesus would have died for nothing (Galatians 2:16–21). Jesus did not abolish the Law, but rather He fulfilled it (Matthew 5:17–18, Luke 18:31–33, Luke 22:37, and John 19:28–30). After Jesus rose from the dead, He spent time with his disciples explaining to them why He had to die in order to fulfill what was written about him in the Law of Moses, the books of the prophets, and the Psalms. He opened their minds so that they could understand the Scriptures and told them *"This is what is written: The Christ will suffer and rise from the dead on the third day, and repentance and forgiveness of sins will be preached in his name to all nations, beginning at Jerusalem"* (Luke 24:46–47). When Jesus said his last words on the cross, *"It is finished"* (John 19:30), He knew He had completed what He had come to do. It would now be possible for men to be saved for eternity if they believed in Him and His finished work on the cross.

Jesus became the sacrifice for sins once and for all so that we no longer need to offer up animals as temporary atonement for our sins (Hebrews 7:27), which was another part of Old Testament Law (Leviticus 1–7). He abolished in His flesh (by His death) the Law, with all its commandments and regulations, and made us fellow citizens with God's people and members of God's household (Ephesians 2:14–20).

Christ is the end of the law so that there may
be righteousness for everyone who believes.
(Romans 10:4)

When you were dead in your sins and in the un-
circumcision of your sinful nature, God made
you alive with Christ. He forgave us all our sins,
having canceled the written code, with its regulations, that was against us and stood opposed
to us; he took it away, nailing it to the cross.
(Colossians 2:13–14)

What, then, was the purpose of the law? It was
added because of transgressions until the Seed
to whom the promise referred had come... But
the Scripture declares that the whole world is
a prisoner of sin, so that what was promised,
being given through faith in Jesus Christ, might
be given to those who believe. Before this faith
came, we were held prisoners by the law, locked
up until faith should be revealed. So the law was
put in charge to lead us to Christ that we might
be justified by faith. Now that faith has come, we
are no longer under the supervision of the law.
(Galatians 3:19, 22–25)

This is why the Law still needs to be taught. People have to
somehow realize that they are sinners and need God's forgiveness. That is why the Law is in charge to lead us to Christ. It is
hard to understand.

But their minds were made dull, for to this day the same veil remains when the old covenant is read. It has not been removed, because only in Christ is it taken away. Even to this day when Moses is read, a veil covers their hearts. But whenever anyone turns to the Lord, the veil is taken away. Now the Lord is the Spirit, and where the Spirit of the Lord is, there is freedom. (2 Corinthians 3:14–17; see also verses 7–18)

To sum it all up, Jesus changed things. That is why there is such a difference in instruction from the Old Testament to the New Testament. Jesus promotes love and forgiveness instead of judgement under the Law.

When the Pharisees, the teachers of the Law, caught a woman committing adultery and brought her to Jesus, they pointed out how the Law of Moses commanded that she be stoned. Jesus knew they were trying to trap him and said, *"If any one of you is without sin, let him be the first to throw a stone at her"* (John 8:7). When nobody condemned her and they all went away, Jesus also did not condemn her, and told her to go and leave her life of sin (John 8:3–11).

Peter came to Jesus one day and asked,

"Lord, how many times shall I forgive my brother when he sins against me? Up to seven times?"

Jesus answered, "I tell you, not seven times, but seventy-seven times." (Matthew 18:21–22)

Jesus then went on to tell the parable of the unmerciful servant who refused to forgive his fellow servant a small debt after he himself had been forgiven a large debt. When the master of the unforgiving servant found out that his servant refused to share the grace he had been granted with his fellow man, he threw him into jail to be tormented until he could pay back what he owed. Jesus said, *"This is how my heavenly Father will treat each of you unless you forgive your brother from your heart"* (Matthew 18:35; see also James 2:12–13).

We will be judged with the same measuring tool that we have used to judge others (Matthew 7:1–2). Therefore, it is crucial that we forgive others and share the mercy and grace that God has lavished on us when He forgave our sins. Our Lord extended his grace towards us in that, *"While we were still sinners, Christ died for us"* (Romans 5:8). Living as a believer is about extending God's grace to others, not hoarding it for ourselves while expecting others to live a perfect life under the Law.

Today, our faith is a matter of the heart. Someday we will all stand before God's judgment seat and give account, not only of our deeds but also our motives and attitudes (1 Corinthians 4:5 and Hebrews 4:12–13). Therefore, I believe that the reason we do things is just as important as the things we actually do.

Jesus wanted our righteousness to surpass that of the Pharisees and teachers of the Law. He said,

> You have heard that it was said to the people long ago, "Do not murder, and anyone who murders will be subject to judgment. But I tell you that anyone who is angry with his brother will be subject to judgement… You have heard that it was said, "Do not commit adultery." But I tell you that anyone who looks at a woman lust-

fully has already committed adultery with her in his heart… You have heard that it was said, "Eye for eye, and tooth for tooth." But I tell you, Do not resist an evil person. If someone strikes you on the right cheek, turn to him the other also. (Matthew 5:21–22, 27–28, 38–39)

This means that we have a higher call, or a bigger responsibility. Jesus instructs us to love our enemies and pray for those who persecute us. He wants us to follow the example of our heavenly Father, who *"causes his sun to rise on the evil and the good, and sends rain on the righteous and the unrighteous"* (Matthew 5:45).

We have been given salvation because of Jesus' sacrifice on the cross. When our righteousness surpasses that of the Pharisees, we are trusting Christ and loving others, not simply following a list of rules. We try to live for the glory of God and the well-being of others—not only to please ourselves and make ourselves look good on the outside.

Paul was a leader who was free in Christ, yet he made himself a slave to everyone for the sake of hopefully winning some to Christ. He became like a Jew to win the Jews, and like a Greek to win the Greeks (1 Corinthians 9:19–22). Although everything was permissible for Paul, not everything was beneficial. He gave up his freedom in Christ to live as others would expect him to, in order not to be a stumbling-block to them (Romans 14 and 1 Corinthians 10:23–33). For example, when Paul took Timothy along on a mission trip, he circumcised him first, because of the Jews, since it was part of the Old Testament Law before Jesus fulfilled it (Acts 16:3). The covenant of circumcision started in Genesis 17, and Paul decided to circumcise Timothy in order to not hinder the faith of the Jews, since they hadn't yet come to the knowledge that Jesus had fulfilled the Law, and that circumcision was no longer necessary.

Jesus was sometimes frustrated by men's interpretation of the Law. When the Pharisees and teachers of the Law asked Jesus why His disciples didn't follow the tradition of the elders, instead of eating their food with unclean hands, He replied, *"You hypocrites! Isaiah was right when he prophesied about you: 'These people honor me with their lips, but their hearts are far from me. They worship me in vain; their teachings are but rules taught by men'"* (Matthew 15:7–9). Elsewhere, He said, *"You have let go of the commands of God and are holding on to the traditions of men"* (Mark 7:8). Isaiah said, *"Woe to those who make unjust laws, to those who issue oppressive decrees, to deprive the poor of their rights and withhold justice from the oppressed of my people, making widows their prey and robbing the fatherless"* (Isaiah 10:1–2).

Many people continue to pick and choose which part of the Law they want to follow. For example, Deuteronomy tells us which kinds of meat people were allowed to eat in Old Testament times (Deuteronomy 14:3–21). It also tells us that women shouldn't wear men's clothing, and vice versa (Deuteronomy 22:5). Many people are very adamant about following the clothing law, but they will eat pork and other meats that were forbidden. James said, *"For whoever keeps the whole law and yet stumbles at just one point is guilty of breaking all of it"* (James 2:10; see also verses 8–13) There is no possible way to keep the whole law. We desperately need Jesus as our Saviour. *"God has bound all men over to disobedience so that he may have mercy on them all"* (Romans 11:32).

The Bible further explains,

> All who rely on observing the law are under a
> curse, for it is written: "Cursed is everyone who
> does not continue to do everything written in
> the Book of the Law." Clearly, no one is justified
> before God by the law, because, "The righteous
> will live by faith." The law is not based on faith;
> on the contrary, "The man who does these things
> will live by them." Christ redeemed us from the
> curse of the law by becoming a curse for us, for
> it is written: "Cursed is everyone who is hung on
> a tree." He redeemed us in order that the bless-
> ing given to Abraham might come to the Gentiles
> through Christ Jesus, so that by faith we might re-
> ceive the promise of the Spirit. (Galatians 3:10–14)

Christ's death redeemed us from the curse of the Law. He
fulfilled the Law's requirements. We now live by faith.

Today we have a new covenant. Jesus died as a ransom to
set us free from the sins committed under the first covenant, and
He is the mediator of this new covenant (Hebrews 9:15). Because
Jesus lives forever, He has a permanent priesthood. Therefore,
He is able to save completely those who come to God through
Him, because He always intercedes for them (Hebrews 7:24–25).
When God promised this covenant, He said, *"I will put my laws
in their minds and write them on their hearts. I will be their God,
and they will be my people. No longer will a man teach his neigh-
bor, or a man his brother, saying, "Know the Lord," because they will
all know me, from the least of them to the greatest. For I will forgive
their wickedness and will remember their sins no more.' By calling*

this covenant 'new,' he has made the first one obsolete; and what is obsolete and aging will soon disappear" (Hebrews 8:10–13; see also Hebrews 7:11–10:18).

This is good news! Today we have a righteousness from God, apart from the Law, which has been made known, to which the Law and the prophets testify. This righteousness from God comes through faith in Jesus Christ to all who believe. There is no difference, *"for all have sinned and fall short of the glory of God, and are justified freely by his grace through the redemption that came by Christ Jesus"* (Romans 3:23–24; see also Acts 13:38–39).

How then shall we live? If following the Law does not make us righteous, and faith in Jesus Christ is the only way to eternal life, how do we know how to live?

Jesus said, *"A new command I give you: Love one another. As I have loved you, so you must love one another. By this all men will know that you are my disciples, if you love one another"* (John 13:34–35). He also told us, *"So in everything, do to others what you would have them do to you, for this sums up the Law and the Prophets"* (Matthew 7:12; see also Luke 6:31).

> An expert in the law, tested him with this question: "Teacher, which is the greatest commandment in the Law?"
>
> Jesus replied: "'Love the Lord your God with all your heart and with all your soul and with all your mind.' This is the first and greatest commandment. And the second is like it: 'Love your neighbor as yourself.' All the Law and Prophets hang on these two commandments." (Matthew 22:35–40)

A guest speaker in our church once explained it this way: "Love God and do what you want." Could it really be that simple? If we love God, we can do whatever we want?

Yes, it really is that simple. Think about it. If I love God, will I make idols to worship in order to arouse His jealousy? If I love my neighbour as myself, will I steal from her, murder her, or have an affair with her husband? If you think about it, all the Law and the prophets really do hang on loving others and treating them the way we hope to be treated.

Paul told us,

> Let no debt remain outstanding, except the continuing debt to love one another, for he who loves his fellowman has fulfilled the law. The commandments, "Do not commit adultery," "Do not murder," "Do not steal," "Do not covet," and whatever other commandment there may be, are summed up in this one rule: "Love your neighbour as yourself." Love does no harm to its neighbour. Therefore love is the fulfillment of the law. (Romans 13:8–10; see also Galatians 5:14)

This is a great encouragement! No longer do we have to worry about trying to keep a law with so many rules. The Holy Spirit inside us fills us with the Lord's love, making it possible for us to live a life of love. The Holy Spirit causes us to rejoice when others come to the saving grace of Jesus, instead of being resentful that they are equally accepted as God's children, just like we were. The person who becomes a Christian later in life has already been punished enough by living through the consequences of a sinful lifestyle, activities which often are detrimental to their health, their family, and their finances.

"The Golden Rule," as the instruction of Matthew 7:12 is often referred to, has been my source of guidance for many occasions when I wasn't sure how to handle a certain situation. I try to put myself in the shoes of the person I'm dealing with and treat them according to how I would hope to be treated if I were in that same situation.

Another scripture that often guides my actions is found in Matthew 25:31–46. It teaches us that whatever we did or didn't do for others—or *"the least of these"*—we have done or failed to do for Jesus. I don't always feel like being nice to strangers, or being hospitable and cooking a meal for someone. This passage reminds me that I am serving Jesus when I choose to obey. It often gives me the strength to keep going, even when I don't feel like it.

I was quite young when I first started reading the Bible. The part that said *"Love the Lord your God with all your heart and with all your soul and with all your mind"* kind of bothered me (Matthew 22:37, Mark 12:30, and Luke 10:27). I couldn't quite fathom loving anyone more than my parents at that stage of my life. When I got a little older and had a boyfriend, who later became my husband, I couldn't quite imagine loving anyone more than him. Then when those darling little babies arrived, well, there is a special love a person has for their children that only parents understand. I continued to have a slightly guilty feeling whenever I came across this passage of Scripture. I felt I loved others more than God. I feared that if I gave Him all my love, there would be none left for anybody else.

Since then, I have learned that the more you divide love, the more it multiplies. In fact, the Bible teaches that God is love, and that *"anyone who does not love his brother, whom he has seen, cannot love God, whom he has not seen"* (1 John 4:20). I now love God with all my heart, and still love everyone I loved before. I no longer feel guilty for loving others, because the more you love God, the more love will overflow to others and multiply. God planned it that way. He is love. I was very encouraged to read that we show our love to Jesus by loving others. What we do for the least of these, we do for Him.

Changes don't come easily for most people. It is hard to let go of things that we've always done, especially if we were taught that certain traditions had to be followed in order to practice our Christian faith. The early Church struggled with this as well. Some believers who belonged to the Pharisees insisted that the new Gentile converts to the Christian faith needed to be circumcised according to the Law of Moses in order to be saved.

This brought Paul and Barnabas into sharp debate with them, and the Church leadership had a meeting to decide what to do. At the conclusion of Peter's speech, he said, *"Now then, why do you try to test God by putting on the necks of the disciples a yoke that neither we nor our fathers have been able to bear? No! We believe it is through the grace of our Lord Jesus that we are saved, just as they are"* (Acts 15:10–11). The assembly then agreed not to make things difficult for the new Gentile believers (Acts 15:1–35). Instead, they wrote a letter of encouragement to the Gentiles and sent it with Paul and Barnabas, with a few guidelines on how to practice their new faith, still implementing a few Old Testament rules which were beneficial for them.

Life in Christ does give us a lot of freedom, and the Old Testament Law is indeed summed up in doing unto others as we want them to do to us. Our actions matter, but we are not saved by our good works, or through following the rules. The New Testament Church was established on the fact that it is through the grace of our Lord Jesus that we are saved, and this is our bottom line. Even people who have been faithful in following the rules need to repent and turn to Christ in order to be saved, because our own righteousness is as filthy rags before almighty God (Isaiah 64:6 and Romans 3:9–31).

Today, the only thing that counts is faith expressing itself through love (Galatians 5:6). When this happens, the rules get followed without a lot of thought or effort. Let us relax in Him, allowing His bountiful love to flow through us as the Holy Spirit uses our bodies to work and move for His honour and glory. Go ahead, love God and do what you want—love Him with all your heart and stand amazed as He leads you in the way of love!

AUTHOR'S TESTIMONY

AND CONCLUSION

IHAVELOVEDBOOKSANDREADINGFORASLONGAS
I can remember. Even before I learned how to read, I brought
home chapter books from the library and got my mom to read
them to me. It didn't take me long to learn how to read, since it
was my favourite subject at school. By Grade Three, I had finished the Bobsey Twins series and was well into Nancy Drew
and Grace Livingstone Hill books. I often completed a whole
book in a day. During the summer, I didn't have access to our
school library, so I read whatever we had at home. Among them
was *Gone with the Wind*. I also devoured my parents' easy reading version of the New Testament with great interest.

When I was fifteen, my dad became a born-again believer
after experiencing severe spiritual battles and a nervous break-
down. My parents started attending an Evangelical church, and
bought a set of Arthur S. Maxwell's *The Bible Story* series. I started attending church with my parents. After hearing the Gospel
preached a few times, and reading the whole set of Bible stories,
I became a believer.

At the end of Volume 10, there was a written invitation to accept Christ into your heart. I prayed to repent of my sins and accept Jesus Christ into my heart as Saviour and Lord. I was later baptized, became a church member, and married my husband in the same church. We continued to mature and grow for a few more years, then moved elsewhere for work when our oldest son was three years old. The following summer, my dad died of cancer after a winter of illness. We grew closer to the Lord during our time of sorrow.

When we first moved, we attended church in a neighbouring town. My husband Abe started seeing a family counsellor to deal with some of his struggles from growing up in an abusive home. The counsellor, Peter Dyck, also happened to be the pastor at St. Andrew's Anglican Church in Morinville, where we lived. After our third son was born, he told a lady at St. Andrew's, Judy Clarke, about us, a young couple with a new baby who were new in town. Judy loved babies, but was a complete stranger to us. She arranged to come over to see the new baby, and brought three little outfits as a gift. I thought she must be very wealthy to be able to be so generous to strangers. As we got to know Judy and her husband Danny better, we learned that they were just normal people, living in modest housing, working for a living—just like us. They weren't rich, but they were filled with the love of Christ and shared His love with us.

That following summer, the pastor asked Abe to help out with janitorial work during the Church's Children's Festival week, which was kind of like Vacation Bible School (VBS). Since our oldest son was about to start Kindergarten, we decided to send him, so that he might meet some more children his age before school started. We attended the program at the end of that week and slowly started attending church there.

Coming from our Mennonite background, we found St. Andrew's very different from what we were used to. We questioned a lot of the traditional things they did. God, through the Holy Spirit, kept drawing us back week after week. The people loved and accepted us the way we were. Peter's preaching and teaching was sound biblical doctrine. He brought the Bible to life as never before. We often went home and studied to see what was wrong with certain traditions, but couldn't find much about it in the Bible. We came to the conclusion that traditions really don't matter a lot. Every church has some of them, and often they were started as a convenient way of accomplishing a purpose, leading to them becoming habits. More importantly, we grew as we questioned and studied.

We soon realized how little we knew. We learned that as long as Jesus Christ is the foundation or chief cornerstone of a church, that church is part of His body. This makes us family with all other believers, making our denomination irrelevant. We grew and became secure children of God during our time at St. Andrew's. We did not want to leave.

However, God had other plans. Our automotive repair business of two years was struggling financially. An acquaintance in our hometown of La Crete, Alberta offered to buy our assets, if Abe would make a two-year commitment to work for him. We had little choice, since we didn't want to claim bankruptcy and leave our creditors with unpaid debt. The weekend that Abe went to La Crete to discuss details with his new boss, the story of Jonah was preached at church. I got the message—Obey before you get swallowed by a fish! St. Andrew's sent us on our way with blessings and prayers, as missionaries of Christ. We managed to slowly pay our accumulated debt over the next few years, and we didn't file bankruptcy. God was with us and provided, one day and one month at a time. Before leaving Morinville, God laid a burden on my heart to share with others some of the things He had taught us.

He has continued to inspire me over the years, especially when I meet people who have the same questions we did. He has given me the gift of literacy and writing, and I felt I must share in writing so that this message would be available to all. Since I became a believer through a written invitation, I know others can do the same. I felt very inadequate, though, so I took a writing course to get better equipped. During our days of questioning and searching in Morinville, Abe purchased a small, inexpensive concordance. That concordance became the tool that helped me most in my research. It helped me find Scripture references that I barely remembered, even from my childhood reading days. It helped me find the truth in the Bible on many issues and subjects we both struggled with.

We can find people's differing opinions all over the place, but only God's Word really matters. The Bereans in Paul's day eagerly examined the Scriptures to see if what Paul said was true (Acts 17:11). This is also what Peter Dyck encouraged at St. Andrew's. I want to pass on that encouragement to you also. Don't take my word for it. Look up each Scripture reference for yourself and find additional references using your concordance. Trust only the information that comes to you directly from the Bible.

This book has been about fifteen years in the praying, researching, writing, and editing process, and still I am scared to publish it. My biggest fear is that some of it might confuse people more than help. Again, I can't emphasize it enough—study your own Bible and God will give you the answers you seek. I am also scared of publicity, partly afraid of ridicule and persecution, and partly afraid of success. I am not a very public person. I don't want to be anyone's hero or enemy, or publicly recognized. I don't like being the centre of attention. If you are offended by something I wrote, please let me know privately so that you can correct me, or so I can further explain what I meant. If you are encouraged by what I wrote, praise God! The contents of this book are His divine inspiration to me. I do appreciate encouragement, though, as do most people.

I realize that I am a woman, and this has also made me hesitate to publish this book, since women are not permitted to have authority over men, and are encouraged to keep silent (1Timothy 2:12). Women are, however, encouraged to teach the younger women (Titus 2:3–5), and to be submissive helpmates to their husbands (Genesis 2:18–24 and Ephesians 5:22–33). My husband Abe has also inspired my writing, as he has been inspired though the Holy Spirit. Many of my words are Abe's God-given insights that he has shared with me over the years. I have considered being an anonymous writer and using a pen name for the book. However, Abe believes that if we can't sign our name to something, we shouldn't bother doing it, since others need to be able to hold us accountable for our words and actions.

Another example of women in ministry is Philip the Evangelist's four unmarried daughters who prophesied (Acts 21:8–9). God said He would pour out His spirit in the last days, at which time sons, daughters, men, and women would prophesy (Acts 2:17–18). *"Everyone who prophesies speaks to men for their strengthening, encouragement and comfort"* (1 Corinthians 14:3). This is my heart's desire for this book, and why I feel called to share it—for the comfort, strengthening, and encouragement of all who read it.

Having said all that, I want you to know that nothing in this book was meant to offend anyone, though I realize some topics are universal issues and quite controversial. I do realize, though, that it is virtually impossible not to offend others when sharing God's Word. Jesus told us this. He said the world would hate us when we follow Him, because they hated Him first. He warned us that we might get thrown out of the synagogue and be put to death, and the people doing it would think they are offering a service to God (John 15:18–16:4). Paul wrote that everyone who wants to live a godly life in Christ Jesus will be persecuted (2 Timothy 3:12). Therefore, I must put my fear aside and trust in God to carry me through, no matter what happens. Even if one person becomes a believer through my efforts with this book, it will be worth everything I might have to go through.

I have tried to take real-life examples to identify with people where they are at, to bring God's truth to them so that they will understand. Many have had a bad experience or perception of religion and have fallen through the cracks without ever having learned about Jesus Christ and His love for them. My desire is that people will be drawn to Christ as they gain biblical insight into the issues they have been struggling with, the issues that have kept them from seeking after the truth. I pray that hearts and souls will be kindled and rekindled with the fire of the Holy Spirit, as people grow a hunger for the Word of God.

I challenge you again—don't take the word of this woman as the truth. Study your Bible and get the truth imprinted on your heart from God's Word, right from the source. Stand upon the truth of God's Word and let no one sway you by their opinions or false doctrines. As you grow and stand strong, you will find you are no longer swayed by the many winds of teaching, but that you have the firm foundation of Christ and His Word to stand on (Ephesians 4:14–16). This firm foundation, founded on the Word of God, along with the Holy Spirit within you, will empower you to live a victorious Christian life, producing bountiful fruit for the glory of God. May God bless you as you live and shine Christ's light upon others!